W9-BBF-593

River Forest Public Library
735 Lathrop Avenue
River Forest, IL 60305
708-366-5205
May 2019

THE MERMAID COOKBOOK

The Mermaid Cookbook copyright © 2019 by Summersdale Publishers, Ltd. All rights reserved. Printed in China. No part of this book may be used or reproduced in any manner whatsoever without written permission except in the case of reprints in the context of reviews.

Andrews McMeel Publishing
A division of Andrews McMeel Universal
1130 Walnut Street, Kansas City, Missouri 64106

www.andrewsmcmeel.com

First published in 2018 by Summersdale Publishers Ltd.
Part of Octopus Publishing Group Limited
Carmelite House, 50 Victoria Embankment
London, EC4Y 0DZ, UK

All recipes by Alix Carey except for: Mermaid's Purse Mirror Glaze Cake p. 29–31, Wave Cake p. 35–37 by Amy Hunter; Oyster Cookies p. 52–53, Mermaid Cheesecake p.113–115 by Claire Berrisford.

19 20 21 22 23 TEN 10 9 8 7 6 5 4 3 2 1

ISBN: 978-1-4494-9739-2

Library of Congress Control Number: 2018964069

Editor: Jean Z. Lucas
Art Director: Holly Swayne
Production Manager: Carol Coe
Production Editor: Margaret Daniels

ATTENTION: SCHOOLS AND BUSINESSES
Andrews McMeel books are available at quantity discounts with bulk purchase for educational, business, or sales promotional use. For information, please e-mail the Andrews McMeel Publishing Special Sales Department: specialsales@amuniversal.com.

THE
MERMAID
COOKBOOK

ALIX CAREY

Andrews McMeel
PUBLISHING®

For Harley and Harper

 CONTENTS

INTRODUCTION

Welcome to *The Mermaid Cookbook*, where all your under-the-sea wishes are guaranteed to come true in the form of delicious treats. Inside this magical book, you'll find forty-six fun-filled recipes ready to help you bring the mysterious mermaids out of the water and into the kitchen. But before you begin Operation Mermaid, you need to find your oceanic name. So, what are you waiting for? On the next page, you'll be able to identify your fantasy alter-ego and begin your baking adventure into the world of the most mesmerizing aquatic legend of all time.

WHAT IS YOUR MERMAID NAME?

To discover your mermaid name, find the initial of your first name and the month you were born in the lists below. Combine the two and state your new alias aloud with joy as you put on your apron and get ready to dive into this magical mermaid feast.

A - MOONSHINE
B - PEBBLE
C - PEARL
D - AQUATA
E - JEWEL
F - PACIFICA
G - CORAL
H - TREASURE
I - SHIMMERING
J - GLISTENING
K - SASSY
L - SPARKLING
M - GLOSSY
N - LUNA
O - STORMY
P - MELODY
Q - COVE
R - FIERCE
S - BRAVE
T - RADIANT
U - CRYSTAL
V - ROYAL
W - BUBBLE
X - MARINE
Y - BAY
Z - SEA QUEEN

JANUARY - SHORE DREAMER
FEBRUARY - MAGIC SCALES
MARCH - TWILIGHT STAR
APRIL - SEA GLIDER
MAY - EMERALD WATERS
JUNE - AQUA ANGEL
JULY - WHISPER WAVE
AUGUST - GOLDEN GODDESS
SEPTEMBER - SUNSHINE REEF
OCTOBER - TIDE DANCER
NOVEMBER - MOONLIGHT GEM
DECEMBER - GLITTER TAIL

KITCHEN ESSENTIALS

Before we get started, let's take a look at all the essential ingredients and equipment you'll need.

INGREDIENTS

Butter – Unsalted butter is best for baking and it is easiest to use at room temperature, but when you're making pastry, it needs to be cold.

Flour – Most of these recipes call for all-purpose flour, but occasionally, when baking cakes, I advise using self-rising flour.

Sugar – The most important types of sugar for the recipes in this book are superfine sugar, confectioners' sugar, and light brown sugar.

Flavor extracts – A number of recipes in this book require vanilla extract, but there are several others that call for other flavors, such as peppermint, if you wish to use these.

Eggs – Always use large eggs, unless otherwise specified.

Gel food coloring – These are preferred over liquid food colorings because, most importantly, they do not dilute any mixtures and, secondly, you only need to add a few drops to make rich, vibrant colors.

Sprinkles and edible glitter – You'll have a hard task getting through this book without sprinkles and edible glitter. The key cake decorations you will need are: nonpareils (tiny balls made of sugar and starch), edible star sprinkles, edible pearls, sugar crystals, and edible glitter.

Edible candy eyes – A few recipes also use edible eyes to help bring your creations to life. Edible candy eyes can be found in the cake-decorating section of most supermarkets, in cake-decoration shops, or online.

White chocolate – Whether it be for dipping, coating, drizzling, or even baking, white chocolate is a big part of many of these recipes. Of course, you are welcome to use dark or milk chocolate as a replacement, but white chocolate is used widely, as its appearance can be changed easily with food coloring.

Desiccated coconut – To add that tropical touch to many recipes in this book, it's worth making sure your cupboard is well-stocked with this ingredient.

Lemon and lime zest – These are finely grated to help add some fresh flavors to your delicious sweet treats.

Cream cheese – This is used in a number of recipes in the book. Don't worry if you're dairy-free, as you can simply replace dairy cream cheese with soya or other non-dairy options.

EQUIPMENT

Baking pans – You will need at least three flat sheet baking pans, a 9 by 13-inch sheet pan, a jelly roll pan, and an 8-inch square pan.

Cake/cupcake pans – All the cakes in this book are baked in round 7 or 8-inch cake pans and you will need at least two of each (maximum of six). All cupcakes are baked in batches of 12, so you will need a 12-cup muffin pan as well as a 12-cup mini muffin pan.

Candy thermometer – When making confectionery items, mirror glaze, and Italian meringue buttercream, a candy thermometer will make the recipes failsafe and easier to follow.

Parchment paper – The majority of recipes will ask you to line a baking sheet or cake pan, so parchment paper is a necessity. (*Note: this is not to be confused with wax paper, which is not heat resistant and can cause baked goods to stick to it like glue. Parchment paper has a silicon lining and is heat resistant, which prevents any cakes or baked goods from sticking to it.*)

Mixing bowls – An assortment of sizes would be ideal, but as long as you have one heatproof mixing bowl, you'll get through this book just fine.

Piping bags – Piping bags are used throughout this book for piping buttercream, meringues, and batter. You can make your own out of resealable plastic bags by cutting off a small corner. However, these are not as accurate as using a piping bag. Piping bags, especially those with a grip, allow you to pipe with absolute accuracy and precision, so I would always recommend having a large stash in your kitchen drawer.

Piping tips – These come in all shapes and sizes to create a variety of decorations, but I most commonly use the star tips (closed and open), which create decorative swirls and wave patterns, and large round tips for macarons, meringue kisses, cake covering, and creating those all-important mermaid scales.

Icing spatula – The icing spatula is a great tool for creating the mermaid scale effect and covering your large cakes with icing.

Cookie cutters – You will find these in a huge variety of shapes and sizes. You can purchase sets of these cutters in every size possible from most kitchen retailers.

Fondant/chocolate molds – Mermaid tail and seashell molds are used several times throughout this book. You could make the recipes without them, but they do add the perfect finishing touch to any mermaid recipe, so I would recommend using them.

Rolling pin – This is a kitchen necessity for crushing crackers (for a cheesecake crust), as well as rolling out pastry.

Cupcake liners – When making cupcakes, you'll need cupcake liners and you can be as adventurous as you wish with the colors. Blues, greens, turquoise, purples, and pinks, as well as metallic colors, are the perfect choices for these recipes.

Electric hand or stand mixer – While I advocate the use of your own mermaid strength, you'll find using an electric hand or stand mixer much easier and quicker for many of these recipes.

Kitchen scale – Baking is a science and requires precise measurements of ingredients.

Measuring spoons – My baking besties. Avoid using normal tableware to approximate these, as they can vary. This might not sound like much difference, but a sponge cake can crack or sink on as little as a few ounces too much or too little baking powder.

Icing smoother – This may remind you of a large scraper, but it is the perfect tool for creating that perfectly smooth buttercream on all your celebration cakes.

Decorating turntable – A 360-degree rotating table makes frosting cakes a breeze and allows for easy piping, smoothing, and decorating.

CUPCAKES

🐚 HEART OF THE OCEAN CUPCAKES 🐚

*Mermaids are known to love and care for all sea creatures,
making them the true hearts of the ocean.*

Makes: 12   🐚   **Time: 2 hours**   🐚   **Difficulty rating:** ⭐ ⭐

INGREDIENTS

Hearts

* ¾ cup plus 2 tablespoons butter, softened
* ¾ cup plus 2 tablespoons superfine sugar
* 3 eggs
* 1¾ cup self-rising flour
* ¼ teaspoon raspberry flavoring
* Pink gel food coloring

Cupcakes

* ⅔ cup butter, softened
* ⅔ cup superfine sugar
* 3 eggs
* 1⅓ cups self-rising flour
* ¼ teaspoon vanilla extract

Buttercream

* ⅔ cup butter, softened
* 3½ cups confectioners' sugar
* Purple gel food coloring

EXTRA EQUIPMENT

You will need a 12-cup muffin pan, two 8-inch cake pans, 12 cupcake liners, a 1-inch heart-shaped cookie cutter, a piping bag, and a closed-star piping tip.

METHOD

For the hearts:

Preheat the oven to 350°F and line two 8-inch cake pans with parchment paper. Set aside.

Place the butter, sugar, eggs, and flour in a large mixing bowl and beat together until pale and fluffy. Add the raspberry flavoring and a drop of pink gel food coloring, then mix until well combined.

Pour the mixture equally between the two cake pans and bake for 20 to 25 minutes. Let cool.

Once cooled, cut out six hearts from each cake pan using the cookie cutter and set aside.

For the cupcakes:

Keep the oven at 350°F and line a muffin pan with 12 cupcake liners.

Add the butter, sugar, eggs, and flour to a large mixing bowl, and beat together until pale and fluffy. Add the vanilla extract and mix until well combined.

Fill each cupcake liner with batter until two-thirds full, then carefully place a sponge heart into the center of each cupcake, pushing it down until it is almost completely submerged in the batter. Bake in the oven for 20 to 25 minutes, until just browned and springy to touch, then let cool on a wire rack.

For the buttercream:

Blend the butter and confectioners' sugar together until smooth, add a few drops of the purple gel food coloring (enough to make the buttercream a pastel color), and combine.

Fit a piping bag with a closed-star tip, transfer the mixture into the piping bag, and pipe swirls of buttercream on top of the cupcakes.

⋆ MERMAID SCALE CUPCAKES ⋆

Mermaids' scales are most beautiful when they shimmer in the sunlight. Recreate your own edible version with these zingy lemon cupcakes topped with glittering buttercream scales. You can use the buttercream technique on larger cakes, too.

Makes: 12 ⋆ **Time: 2 hours** ⋆ **Difficulty rating:** ★ ★

INGREDIENTS

Cupcakes

- ★ ⅔ cup butter, softened
- ★ ⅔ cup plus 2 teaspoons light brown sugar
- ★ 3 eggs
- ★ 1⅓ cups self-rising flour
- ★ Zest of 1 lemon

Buttercream

- ★ ¾ cup plus 2 tablespoons butter, softened
- ★ 3½ cups confectioners' sugar
- ★ Zest of 1 lemon
- ★ Gel food coloring of your choice
- ★ Edible silver glitter

EXTRA EQUIPMENT

You will need a 12-cup muffin pan, 12 cupcake liners, a piping bag, a round-hole piping tip, and a small icing spatula.

METHOD

For the cupcakes:

Preheat the oven to 350°F and line a muffin pan with 12 cupcake liners. Set aside.

Place the butter, sugar, eggs, and flour in a large mixing bowl, and beat together until pale and fluffy. Add the lemon zest and mix until well combined.

Fill each cupcake liner with batter until two-thirds full and bake in the oven for 20 to 25 minutes, until just browned and springy to touch.

Remove from the oven and let cool on a wire rack.

For the buttercream:

Blend the butter and confectioners' sugar together until smooth, add the lemon zest and several drops of gel food coloring (enough to make the buttercream a vibrant color), and combine.

Fit a piping bag with a round-hole tip, transfer the buttercream mixture into the piping bag, and pipe one row of dots along the top of the cupcake.

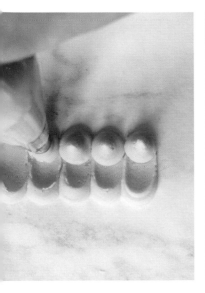  

Using the back of a teaspoon or a small icing spatula, spread the buttercream dots out to create the appearance of a scale. Repeat both steps on the next row and the row after until you have completely covered the cupcake.

Finish with a sprinkle of edible silver glitter and serve.

🐚 OCTOPUS CUPCAKES 🐚

Octopuses spread so much love to their underwater friends that they need three hearts to contain it. These squishy, cute octopus cupcakes are guaranteed to make your heart melt.

Makes: 12 🐚 **Time: 2 hours** 🐚 **Difficulty rating:** ⭐ ⭐

INGREDIENTS

Cupcakes

- ⅔ cup butter, softened
- ⅔ cup plus 2 teaspoons light brown sugar
- 3 eggs
- 1⅓ cups self-rising flour
- ⅓ cup desiccated coconut

Buttercream

- ¾ cup plus 2 tablespoons butter, softened
- 3½ cups confectioners' sugar
- 1 teaspoon vanilla extract
- Turquoise gel food coloring

Octopuses

- 7 ounces white chocolate
- Orange gel food coloring
- 12 white marshmallows
- 24 edible candy eyes

EXTRA EQUIPMENT

You will need a 12-cup muffin pan, 12 cupcake liners, a closed-star piping tip, a writing-tip piping tip, and two piping bags.

METHOD

For the cupcakes:

Preheat the oven to 350°F and line a muffin pan with 12 cupcake liners. Set aside.

Place the butter, sugar, eggs, and flour in a large mixing bowl and beat together until pale and fluffy. Add the desiccated coconut and mix until well combined.

Fill each cupcake liner with batter until two-thirds full and bake in the oven for 20 to 25 minutes, until just browned and springy to touch.

Remove from the oven and let cool on a wire rack.

For the buttercream:

Blend the butter and confectioners' sugar together until smooth, add the vanilla extract and a drop of turquoise gel food coloring (enough to make the buttercream a pale green tone), and combine.

Fit a piping bag with a closed-star tip, transfer the buttercream mixture into the piping bag, and pipe swirls on top of each cupcake.

For the octopuses:

Prepare a baking sheet with parchment paper and set aside.

Place the white chocolate in a heatproof bowl over a saucepan of simmering water. Let the chocolate melt completely, stirring occasionally, then add ¼ teaspoon orange gel food coloring and stir. Take the bowl off the heat and let the chocolate cool slightly.

When the chocolate is cool enough to hold your finger in without burning it, you can begin dipping your marshmallows. Pierce the end of a marshmallow with a fork or a toothpick and dip it into the orange-colored chocolate, coating it fully. Remove the marshmallow from the fork and let it sit on the baking sheet to set a little. Continue the previous steps with the remaining marshmallows.

Stick the candy eyes to the chocolate-coated marshmallows while the chocolate is still sticky, then carefully place them on top of the buttercream once the chocolate has completely set.

Place the remaining orange chocolate into a piping bag fitted with a writing tip and pipe the octopus arms on either side of the marshmallow and down the sides of the buttercream.

Let set completely, then serve.

🐚 DIVE INTO THE OCEAN CUPCAKES 🐚

Create a splash with these simple-to-make but beautifully detailed lime-flavored mermaid cupcakes.

Makes: 12 🐚 **Time: 2 hours** 🐚 **Difficulty rating:** ⭐⭐

INGREDIENTS

Cupcakes

* ⅔ cup butter, softened
* ⅔ cup plus 2 teaspoons light brown sugar
* 3 eggs
* 1⅓ cups self-rising flour
* Zest of 1 lime

Buttercream

* ¾ cup plus 2 tablespoons butter, softened
* 3½ cups confectioners' sugar
* Zest of 1 lime
* Turquoise and purple gel food coloring
* Edible silver glitter

Decorations

* 7 ounces white chocolate
* ¼ cup brown sugar
* Edible pearl sprinkles

EXTRA EQUIPMENT

You will need a 12-cup muffin pan, 12 cupcake liners, two medium-sized piping bags, a large piping bag, a closed-star piping tip, a small mermaid tail mold, and seashell molds.

METHOD

For the cupcakes:

Preheat the oven to 350°F and line a muffin pan with 12 cupcake liners. Set aside.

Place the butter, sugar, eggs, and flour in a large mixing bowl, and beat together until pale and fluffy. Add the lime zest and mix until well combined.

Fill each cupcake liner with batter until two-thirds full and bake in the oven for 20 to 25 minutes, until just browned and springy to touch.

Remove from the oven and let cool on a wire rack.

For the buttercream:

Blend the butter and confectioners' sugar together until smooth, add the lime zest, and combine.

Split the mixture equally between two bowls, adding 1 to 2 drops purple gel food coloring to one bowl and 1 to 2 drops turquoise gel food coloring to the other, mixing each until your frosting reaches a pastel tone.

Fill two piping bags with the buttercream, one for each color, then cut the ends and place both into a larger piping bag fitted with a closed-star tip.

Pipe swirls of the buttercream onto each cupcake.

For the decorations:

Break the white chocolate into small pieces, place them in a heatproof bowl over a saucepan of simmering water, and, stirring occasionally, let the chocolate melt down completely.

Split the melted chocolate equally into three bowls and color one turquoise, one purple—using 1 to 2 drops of food coloring for each—and leave the other plain.

Fill the mermaid and seashell molds with a little amount from each of the bowls of chocolate, then mix it around a little with a toothpick. Put the molds in the freezer to set hard for 5 minutes.

Repeat until you have enough decorations for all 12 cupcakes, then carefully place the mermaid tails on top of each of the cupcakes and place one or two chocolate shells next to it. Finish with a dusting of brown sugar and a few pearl sprinkles, and serve.

🐚 CORAL REEF BUTTERCREAM 🐚

In the summer months, mermaids migrate to Italy for the warm weather, but also to taste the silky Italian meringue buttercream for which the country is renowned.

Makes: Enough to frost 12 cupcakes 🐚 **Time: 45 minutes** 🐚
Difficulty rating: ⭐ ⭐ ⭐

INGREDIENTS

* ½ cup water
* 1⅓ cups superfine sugar, divided
* 5 large egg whites
* 2¼ cups butter, softened
* Pinch of salt
* 1 teaspoon vanilla extract
* Gel food coloring (orange, purple, yellow and green)

EXTRA EQUIPMENT

You will need a candy thermometer, an electric hand mixer, 4 piping bags, a closed-star piping tip, an open-star piping tip, a grass piping tip, and a small petal piping tip.

METHOD

This is quite a complicated set of instructions where timing and advance planning are everything, but once you've made one batch of buttercream, you'll realize that it's actually quite straightforward.

Before you begin making the buttercream, bake 12 cupcakes using the exact ingredients and method for the Mermaid Scale Cupcakes on page 18.

First, pour the water into a saucepan and add 1 cup plus 3 tablespoons of the superfine sugar. On medium heat, stir the ingredients until the sugar dissolves to create a syrup. Then place your thermometer in the pan and bring the mixture to a boil without stirring it. Now turn your attention to the egg whites.

Prepare a large bowl of cold water and set it to one side near the stove for later.

In another large bowl, begin beating the egg whites with an electric hand mixer until they hold stiff peaks. Gradually mix in the remaining superfine sugar and continue for 5 minutes, until the mixture can be held upside down without falling out of the bowl. Now you have meringue.

Returning to your syrup, check the temperature and as soon as it reaches 250°F, remove the pan from the heat and plunge the base of it into the bowl of cold water for 3 seconds. This stops the mixture from getting any hotter.

Next, gradually pour the syrup in a thin stream into your meringue mix, gently beating on low speed all the while. Be careful when pouring, as if the liquid strays too close to the edge of the bowl, it will set there, and if it's poured over the moving beaters, the hot syrup may spray everywhere. Continue beating the mixture for 8 to 10 minutes, until the bowl feels just lukewarm.

The next stage is to gradually beat in the butter, followed by the salt and vanilla extract. The mixture may look like it has curdled at first, but as you continue to beat it, it will form a smooth buttercream.

Split the mixture equally between four bowls and add ¼ teaspoon of gel food coloring to each bowl so you have four pastel shades of buttercream. Using four piping bags, fit each one with a different piping tip. Add orange buttercream to the closed-star tip bag, purple buttercream to the open-star tip bag, green buttercream to the petal tip bag, and yellow buttercream to the grass tip bag.

Start by piping the orange swirls on each cupcake, followed by the purple, then fill the gaps with the yellow and green.

CELEBRATION CAKES

❦ MERMAID'S PURSE MIRROR ❦ GLAZE CAKE

The mermaids' purses you find washed up on the beach are actually the egg cases of sharks and rays. This mermaid's purse cake is a shimmering reflection of their deep purple hue and, what's more, it's edible!

Serves: 12 to 16 ❦ **Time: 2 hours plus overnight freezing for the cake; 1 hour 30 minutes for the Mermaid Kisses** ❦ **Difficulty rating: ★ ★ ★**

INGREDIENTS

Cake

* 1⅔ cups self-rising flour
* ¾ cup plus 2 tablespoons butter, softened
* ¾ cup plus 2 tablespoons superfine sugar
* 3 eggs
* ½ teaspoon baking powder
* ½ teaspoon vanilla extract

Buttercream

* ¾ cup plus 2 tablespoons butter, softened
* 3½ cups confectioners' sugar

Glaze

* 1½ packets unflavored gelatin powder
* 9 tablespoons lukewarm water, divided

* ¾ cup granulated sugar
* ⅓ cup plus 2 tablespoons glucose syrup (or corn syrup)
* ¼ cup plus 3 tablespoons sweetened condensed milk
* 5 ounces white chocolate chips
* Purple gel food coloring

Decorations

* Dark chocolate chips
* Mermaid Kisses (page 60). These take approximately 1 hour and 30 minutes to make. They can be stored in an airtight container for 7 to 10 days if you wish to make them ahead of baking the cake.
* Handful of blackberries and blueberries

EXTRA EQUIPMENT

You will need two 8-inch cake pans, an 8-inch diameter cake board, an icing spatula, an immersion blender, a candy thermometer, and a toothpick.

METHOD

For the cake:

Preheat the oven to 350°F and line two 8-inch cake pans with parchment paper. Set aside.

Mix the flour, butter, sugar, eggs, baking powder, and vanilla in a bowl and beat together until smooth, pale, and fluffy, then fill the two cake pans with batter, making sure they're level, and bake for 20 minutes.

Remove from the oven and let cool in the pans for 15 minutes before lifting out and placing on a wire rack to cool completely.

For the buttercream:

Combine the butter and confectioners' sugar and mix until smooth, pale, and fluffy.

Assembling the cake:

Assemble the cake by adding a little white buttercream to an 8-inch cake board and placing one of the layers on top. Add 2 tablespoons of buttercream to the top of the layer, spread it out across the entire surface, and then add the second layer on top of the first.

Cover the entire cake with a thick layer of buttercream and smooth it out with an icing spatula and icing smoother. To smooth your buttercream, take your icing smoother, holding it lightly on the cake with the bottom touching the turntable, and rotate the cake. If you need to go around the cake again, clean your icing smoother and repeat. The smoother your buttercream looks at this stage, the better finish you will get with the mirror glaze. (*Note: mirror glaze works better on a frozen cake, so ideally you want to freeze the cake overnight before adding the glaze.*)

For the glaze:

Stir the gelatin into 4 tablespoons of the lukewarm water in a small bowl and set aside for later.

In a saucepan, boil the sugar, remaining 5 tablespoons water, and syrup until it reaches 217°F. Take the pan off the heat and whisk in the gelatin. Then whisk the sweetened condensed milk into the mixture.

Add the contents of the pan to a heatproof bowl with white chocolate chips and your gel food coloring—enough to make the chocolate a vibrant purple—and gently stir the mixture very briefly. Then blend for about 1 to 2 minutes. You don't want to add air to the mixture, so try not to move the blender too much.

Let the mixture cool to around 86–90°F, gently stirring occasionally to prevent a skin from forming and popping any air bubbles on the surface with a toothpick.

It is best to check the consistency of your glaze before pouring it onto the cake by using the back of a spoon. If the glaze covers and sticks to the back of the spoon, with a small amount of runoff, then it is the perfect pouring temperature. If your glaze is too cold and stiff, put it in the microwave or on the stove for a few seconds.

When you are ready to use the glaze, take your frozen cake from the freezer and put it on top of a wire rack so that the excess glaze can drain through. Pouring mirror glaze is very messy, so a good tip is to put a pan underneath the wire rack to catch the excess.

Pour the mirror glaze over the cake, ensuring the top and sides are completely covered. Any excess on the top can be wiped away using an icing spatula.

Let the glaze dry before decorating.

For the decorations:
Scatter the dark chocolate chips around the base of the cake and place Mermaid Kisses on top of the cake, along with a handful of blueberries and blackberries.

🐚 MERMAID KISSES CAKE 🐚

Baking this cake requires a big heart and a caring soul. The difficulty is finding the elusive mermaids to help top it off with their kisses!

Serves: 10 to 12 🐚 **Time: 2 to 3 hours** 🐚 **Difficulty rating:** ★ ★

INGREDIENTS

Cake

* 2⅔ cups self-rising flour
* 1⅓ cups butter, softened
* 1⅓ cups superfine sugar
* 6 eggs
* 1 teaspoon baking powder
* 1 teaspoon vanilla extract

Buttercream

* 2¼ cups butter, softened
* 8⅔ cups confectioners' sugar
* 1 teaspoon vanilla extract
* Turquoise gel food coloring

Decorations

* Mermaid Kisses (page 60). These take approximately 1 hour and 30 minutes to make. They can be stored in an airtight container for 7 to 10 days if you wish to make them ahead of baking the cake.

EXTRA EQUIPMENT

You will need two 7-inch cake pans, an 8-inch diameter cake board, an icing spatula, an icing smoother, and a decorating turntable.

METHOD

For the cake:

Preheat the oven to 350°F and line two 7-inch cake pans with parchment paper. Set aside.

Place the flour, butter, sugar, eggs, baking powder, and vanilla extract in a bowl and whisk together for 2 to 3 minutes, until smooth, pale, and fluffy.

Divide the cake batter between the two lined cake pans and bake for 25 to 30 minutes.

Remove from the oven and let cool in the pans for 15 minutes before lifting out and placing on a wire rack to cool completely. Once cool, cut the two sponge cakes in half horizontally, so you have four layers ready for assembling.

For the buttercream:

Place the butter in a bowl and beat until smooth, then add the confectioners' sugar and vanilla extract and continue mixing until smooth and pale.

Add a drop of turquoise gel food coloring, enough to create a mint green tone, and mix thoroughly.

To assemble:

Add a little buttercream to the 8-inch cake board so that your first cake layer can be secured to the base. Continue sandwiching the remaining cake layers, with a generous portion of the mint green buttercream in between each layer.

Cover the entire cake with a thin layer of the mint green buttercream and smooth it out with an icing spatula, then leave in the fridge for an hour to harden.

Add a second, thicker coat of the mint green buttercream, then use an icing spatula to smooth it around. Place the cake on the decorating turntable, take your icing smoother, holding it lightly on the cake with the bottom touching the turntable, and rotate the cake. If you need to go around the cake again, clean your icing smoother and repeat.

Cover the cake in Mermaid Kisses.

❧ WAVE CAKE ❧

If you like making waves in the kitchen, this recipe is for you. Surprise your guests when you cut into the cake and reveal its different shades of the ocean.

Serves: 20　❧　**Time: 2 to 3 hours**　❧　**Difficulty rating:** ★ ★

INGREDIENTS

Cake

- ★ 4⅓ cups plus 1 tablespoon self-rising flour
- ★ 2¼ cups butter, softened
- ★ 2¼ cups superfine sugar
- ★ 6 eggs
- ★ 1 teaspoon baking powder
- ★ 1 teaspoon vanilla extract
- ★ Blue gel food coloring

Buttercream

- ★ 1¾ cups butter, softened
- ★ 7 cups confectioners' sugar
- ★ Blue gel food coloring
- ★ White gel food coloring (optional)

EXTRA EQUIPMENT

You will need three 8-inch cake pans, six mixing bowls, a 10-inch diameter cake board, an icing spatula, an icing smoother, and a decorating turntable.

METHOD

For the cake:

Preheat the oven to 350°F and line the 8-inch cake pans with parchment paper. Set aside. (This cake will need to be baked in two batches unless you have a very big oven.)

Place the flour, butter, sugar, eggs, baking powder, and vanilla extract in a bowl, and mix together until smooth, pale, and fluffy. You may want to add half the ingredients to one bowl and the other half to another to make it easier to mix.

Split the batter equally between six bowls and add blue gel food coloring to five of them, ensuring they are different shades of blue, ranging from pale to dark. Add the food coloring in very small amounts so you are able to achieve a good range of blues.

Fill three cake pans with three of the six batters, making sure they are level, then place the pans into the preheated oven and bake for 20 minutes, or until you can insert a toothpick into the cake and it comes out clean.

Remove from the oven and let cool in the pans for 15 minutes before lifting out and placing on a wire rack to cool completely.

Repeat the baking instructions with the remaining three bowls of batter, starting with washing and preparing the pans.

For the buttercream:

Combine the butter and confectioners' sugar and mix until smooth, pale, and fluffy. Separate a third of the mixture into a bowl and color with blue gel food coloring until nice and vibrant. The rest of the buttercream might look a little yellow, so you may wish to add a little white gel food coloring to the remaining buttercream, but this is optional.

Assembling the cake:

Layer the cake together by adding a little white buttercream to a 10-inch cake board and sticking the darkest blue layer onto it. Add a tablespoon of buttercream to the top of the cake layer and spread it out across the entire surface, then add the next darkest blue cake. Repeat and continue with the other blue cakes, pregressively getting lighter for each layer. Set the plain colored cake aside for decoration later.

Cover the entire cake with a thin layer of buttercream and smooth it out with an icing spatula. Leave in the fridge for 1 hour, until the buttercream has hardened.

To create the ombre effect:

Set your cake on a decorating turntable and, starting at the bottom, spread the blue frosting using your icing spatula so that it covers the side of the cake halfway up. Once you reach the middle of the cake, spread the white frosting and the blue frosting alternately, cleaning your spatula in between. Don't worry about being neat at this stage or if the colors start mixing together. As you move toward the top of the cake, spread the white frosting around the cake. You do not need to use lots of frosting for this, but enough so that when you smooth it out, there will be no cake showing through.

Once all the colors have been blended together with an icing spatula, it's time to smooth them together using an icing smoother. For best results, place the icing smoother edge lightly on the cake, with the bottom touching the turntable, and rotate the cake around, continuing until the surface is smooth. If you need to go around the cake again, clean your icing smoother and repeat. If you can see the cake through the frosting, add more frosting to the area and repeat with the icing smoother.

For the top:

Randomly add white and blue buttercream blobs onto the top of the cake with your icing spatula so that the entire surface is covered. Using your spatula, swirl patterns in the buttercream on top so that the two colors mix together and create a wave effect.

For the decoration:

Either using your hands or a blender, crush the reserved plain colored cake layer into crumbs so that it resembles sand. Using the remaining buttercream, stick the cake crumbs to the cake board next to the bottom of the cake.

⚜ ULTIMATE DIVING MERMAID CAKE ⚜

One taste of this gorgeous lemon showstopper and you'll be diving in for more.

Serves: 10 to 12 ⚜ Time: 2 to 3 hours ⚜ Difficulty rating: ★ ★

INGREDIENTS

Cake

* ★ 3½ cups self-rising flour
* ★ 1¾ cups butter, softened
* ★ 1¾ cups superfine sugar
* ★ 6 eggs
* ★ 1 teaspoon baking powder
* ★ Zest of 1 lemon

Italian meringue buttercream

* ★ ½ cup water
* ★ 1⅓ cups superfine sugar
* ★ 5 large egg whites
* ★ 2¼ cups butter, softened
* ★ Pinch of salt
* ★ Zest of 1 lemon
* ★ Gel food coloring (orange, purple, and turquoise)

Decorations

* ★ 2 ounces white chocolate
* ★ Gold sugar crystals

EXTRA EQUIPMENT

You will need two 7-inch cake pans, an 8-inch diameter cake board, an icing spatula, an icing smoother, a decorating table, three piping bags, two open-star piping tips, a closed-star piping tip, and a mermaid tail mold.

METHOD

For the cake:

Preheat the oven to 350°F and line two 7-inch cake pans with parchment paper. Set aside.

Place the flour, butter, sugar, eggs, baking powder, and lemon zest in a bowl and whisk together for 2 to 3 minutes, until smooth, pale, and fluffy.

Divide the cake batter between the two lined cake pans and bake for 20 to 25 minutes.

Remove from the oven and let cool in the pans for 15 minutes before lifting out and placing on a wire rack to cool completely. When cool, cut the two cake layers in half horizontally so you have four layers ready for assembling.

For the Italian meringue buttercream:

Follow steps 3 through 8 for Coral Reef Buttercream on pages 25–26 to make the Italian meringue buttercream, replacing the vanilla extract with lemon zest. Then split the mixture equally between two bowls, coloring one half a light mint green with a drop of turquoise gel food coloring. Split the other half between two bowls and add a drop of the purple gel food coloring to one bowl and a drop of the orange gel food coloring to the other bowl, and mix until well combined.

Assembling and decorating the cake:

Melt the white chocolate in a bowl set over a saucepan of simmering water, or in a microwave. Add 1 to 2 drops of orange gel food coloring and stir to combine. Fill a mermaid tail mold. Leave in the fridge to set. Repeat until you have two mermaid tails ready for decoration.

Add a little buttercream to the 8-inch cake board so that your first cake layer can be secured to the base. Continue sandwiching the remaining layers with a generous portion of the mint green buttercream in between each layer.

Cover the entire cake with a thin layer of the green buttercream and smooth it out with an icing spatula, then leave in the fridge for 1 hour to harden.

Add a second, thicker coat of the mint green buttercream (setting a few tablespoons aside for piping later), then use an icing spatula to smooth it around. Take your icing smoother and place it lightly on the cake, with the bottom touching the turntable, and rotate the cake. If you need to go around the cake again, clean your icing smoother and repeat.

Add the three different colored buttercreams to three separate piping bags, using the closed-star tip for the green buttercream, and the open-star tips for the orange and purple buttercream.

Pipe different colored swirls onto the top and down one of the sides of the cake, add the two orange chocolate mermaid tails on top and a dusting of gold sugar crystals, then serve.

🐚 SANDCASTLE SHOWSTOPPER 🐚

A trip to the beach is not complete without building a sandcastle. Now, with the help of a little mermaid magic, you can create your own edible version. This recipe has many layers and stages, but masterpieces are worth the time and effort, and, more importantly, it tastes incredible.

Serves: 25 to 30   🐚   **Time: 3 hours**   🐚   **Difficulty rating:** ★ ★ ☆

INGREDIENTS

Cake

* ★ 5⅓ cups self-rising flour
* ★ 2⅔ cups butter, softened
* ★ 2⅔ cups superfine sugar
* ★ 12 eggs
* ★ 2 teaspoons baking powder
* ★ 14 ounces fresh raspberries
* ★ 2 teaspoons vanilla extract

Buttercream

* ★ 4⅓ cups plus 1 tablespoon butter, softened
* ★ 17⅓ cups plus 1 tablespoon confectioners' sugar
* ★ 2 teaspoons vanilla extract

Filling

* ★ 1¾ cups raspberry jam

Edible sand

* ★ 1½ cups plus 3 tablespoons graham crackers (or 13½ graham cracker sheets)
* ★ ⅓ cup plus 2 tablespoons soft brown sugar

Decorations

* ★ 2 ice cream cones
* ★ ¼ cup plus 1 tablespoon pink fondant, or 3½ ounces
* ★ ¼ cup plus 1 tablespoon orange fondant, or 3½ ounces
* ★ 3½ ounces white chocolate (optional)

EXTRA EQUIPMENT

You will need two 8-inch cake pans, two 6-inch cake pans, a 6-inch diameter cake board, a 10-inch diameter cake board, an icing spatula, an icing smoother, a piping bag, a large round piping tip, a decorating turntable, four dowel rods, a serrated knife, a cake lifter, a food processor, two thick paper straws, a small round piping tip, and seashell molds.

METHOD

(*Note: the pinwheel decorations should ideally be made ahead of time, as they need to dry out overnight before they are secured onto the cake.*)

For the cake:

Preheat the oven to 350°F and line two 8-inch cake pans and two 6-inch cake pans with parchment paper. Set aside.

Place the flour, butter, sugar, eggs, and baking powder in a large bowl and whisk together for 2 to 3 minutes, until smooth, pale, and fluffy.

In a separate bowl, crush the raspberries with a fork, leaving some whole, then add them to the cake batter with the vanilla extract and gently fold them in.

Divide the cake batter between all four lined cake pans and bake the 8-inch cakes for 30 to 35 minutes and the 6-inch cakes for 20 minutes.

Remove from the oven and leave in the pans for 15 minutes before lifting the cakes out and placing them on a wire rack to cool completely. Once cool, cut the four sponge cakes in half horizontally, so you have eight layers ready for assembling.

For the buttercream:

Place the butter in a bowl and beat until smooth, then gradually add the confectioners' sugar and vanilla extract and mix together until smooth and pale.

Assembling the cake:

Add a little buttercream to the 6-inch cake board and place one 6-inch cake layer onto it (set aside the layer with the smoothest surface and use last). Add ¼ cup of raspberry jam and place the remaining 6-inch cake layers on top, alternating between jam and cake.

Fit a piping bag with the large round piping tip and fill the bag with buttercream. Cover the entire 6-inch cake with a thin layer of buttercream and smooth it out with an icing spatula, then leave in the fridge for 1 hour to harden.

Follow the same steps for the 8-inch cake, but use the 10-inch cake board and ⅓ cup of jam between the layers.

Add a second, thicker coat of the buttercream to both cakes, then use an icing spatula to smooth it around as best as you can. Place one of the cakes on the decorating turntable, then take your icing smoother, holding it lightly against the cake with the bottom touching the turntable, and slowly rotate the cake. If you need to go around the cake again to make it smoother, clean your icing smoother and repeat. Then repeat this with the other cake.

To stack the cakes, insert the four dowel rods close to the center of the 8-inch cake, so the 6-inch cake covers them.

To cut your dowel rods to size, use a pencil to mark the height of the cake on one of them and then lift it out and cut it at the pencil mark with a serrated knife. (*Note: it's important that the top of the dowel rod sits flush with the top of the cake so that the cake you layer on top has something to sit on*.) Discard or put the rest of the dowel rod to one side, so you know which one you should use.

Remove the rest of the dowels from the cake and, using the first dowel as a guide, cut them to equal size. Sand the tips down to smooth them out and avoid splintering, then insert all four dowels back into the cake. Using a cake lifter, carefully stack the 6-inch tier on top. Don't worry if you get a few finger marks in the buttercream as you can smooth this back out when the cake is stacked and in position.

For the edible sand:

Place the graham crackers and sugar in a food processor and pulse until the graham crackers are very fine crumbs.

While the buttercream is still wet, take handfuls of the edible sand (making sure you leave some of the graham cracker mixture for the decorations) and gently press it onto the two tiers of the cake until they are fully covered.

For the decorations:

Coat two ice cream cones with buttercream, position them on the back of the top tier of the cake, and cover with the remaining edible sand mixture.

For the polka-dot pinwheel, roll out the orange fondant to ¼-inch thickness and cut out a 4-inch by 4-inch square.

Roll out the pink fondant to ¼-inch thickness and, using the round piping tip, cut out around ten small circles. Press the pink circles into the orange fondant square in a random formation.

Repeat the process with the remaining fondant, but reverse the colors (orange dots on pink fondant), or you could create a striped pinwheel by using a rolling pin to press strips of one of the fondants into the other 4-inch by 4-inch fondant. (*Note: always make sure that the 'finished' fondant is a perfect square— otherwise creating the pinwheel shape won't work.*)

Using your knife, make four diagonal slits, starting at each corner of the fondant and finishing approximately ¾ inch from the center of the fondant.

Wet the center of the fondant slightly with a little water and place the tip of one of the straws on top of it. This will be your pinwheel handle.

Pick up one corner of the fondant and bend it inward so that the tip reaches the center. Press it down so it sticks to the fondant center and covers a section of the straw.

Repeat with the three other corners until you have the pinwheel shape, then roll a small ball of fondant and stick it to the center to cover where all the corners meet.

Repeat these steps with the other fondant square and straw.

Let the fondant dry out overnight, then, when ready, insert one pinwheel into the bottom tier and another into the top tier.

As a final touch, decorate with white chocolate shells made by melting 3½ ounces of white chocolate in a bowl set over a saucepan of simmering water. Fill the seashell molds with the white chocolate and leave in the fridge to set hard for 20 minutes. When ready, carefully remove the chocolates from the molds and decorate at the base of each tier for a realistic sandcastle effect.

COOKIES

🐚 JAM CLAMS 🐚

Take a bite of these buttery clams and discover a hidden pearl upon a bed of delicious strawberry jam.

Makes: 10 🐚 Time: 45 minutes 🐚 Difficulty rating: ⭐

INGREDIENTS

Cookies

- ★ 1 cup plus 2 tablespoons butter, softened
- ★ ⅓ cup plus 3 tablespoons confectioners' sugar
- ★ 2 teaspoons vanilla extract
- ★ 2 cups plus 1 tablespoon all-purpose flour
- ★ 6 tablespoons cornstarch
- ★ 2 to 3 tablespoons milk

Filling

- ★ 10 tablespoons strawberry jam
- ★ 3 tablespoons plus 1 teaspoon white fondant icing
- ★ Confectioners' sugar, for dusting

EXTRA EQUIPMENT

You will need a piping bag and an open-star piping tip.

METHOD

For the cookies:

Preheat the oven to 350°F and line two baking sheets with parchment paper. Set aside.

Place the butter and confectioners' sugar in a large bowl and beat with a whisk until pale and fluffy. Add the vanilla extract and beat again until well incorporated.

Sift in the flour and cornstarch, then fold them into the butter mixture using a spatula until combined. Add the milk, a little at a time, and mix thoroughly (the dough should feel sticky).

Spoon the dough into a piping bag fitted with a large open-star piping tip.

Pipe swirls about 2 inches in diameter onto two baking sheets, leaving 1 inch between swirls.

Bake for 10 to 12 minutes, until they are a pale golden color and cooked through. Let cool on the baking sheets for a few minutes before transferring to cool fully on a wire rack.

For the filling:

While the cookies are cooling, make your fondant pearls by rolling out a 1-teaspoon piece of fondant into a smooth ball. You want to make ten pearls in total.

When the cookies are cool, pair them up and turn one half upside down so the flat side is facing up. Spoon a tablespoon of jam onto the flat side and lay a fondant pearl toward the front. Top with the other cookie, resting it on top of the jam and pearl at an angle to make it look like it is slightly open. Sprinkle with a dusting of confectioners' sugar.

Repeat with the remaining cookies and serve.

🐚 SEA HOLLY SHORTBREAD 🐚

If you can't find any sea holly growing along the coast or on the dunes when you next visit the beach, try making these cookie versions in your kitchen instead. Very delicious and definitely not spiky.

Makes: 12 to 14 🐚 **Time: 2 hours 30 minutes** 🐚 **Difficulty rating:** ⭐

INGREDIENTS

Shortbread

* ⅓ cup plus 2 tablespoons salted butter
* 3 tablesoons confectioners' sugar
* 1¼ cups all-purpose flour, plus more for dusting
* 3 tablespoons cornstarch

Icing

* 1 (14-ounce) package royal icing mix
* 3 to 4 tablespoons water
* Blue gel food coloring

EXTRA EQUIPMENT

You will need a 2½-inch star cutter, two piping bags, and a writing-tip piping tip.

METHOD

For the shortbread:

Preheat the oven to 350°F and line a baking sheet with parchment paper. Set aside.

In a large bowl, combine the butter and sugar together until soft and fluffy, then add the flour and cornstarch and stir until the mixture forms a firm dough.

Place the dough on a lightly floured surface and knead gently until smooth, then roll out to a thickness of ¼ inch.

Using a 2½-inch star cutter, cut out 14 cookies and arrange them on the baking sheet, spaced slightly apart, then chill in the fridge for 30 minutes.

Bake for 10 to 15 minutes, until lightly golden, then allow to cool for 5 minutes before transferring to a wire rack to cool completely.

For the icing:

Place the royal icing mix in a large mixing bowl and stir in water until it reaches the consistency of toothpaste. Split the mixture between two bowls and add a drop of the blue gel food coloring to one bowl to create a light blue color.

Set the bowl of white icing to one side.

Split the light blue icing mixture in half again, and in one of the bowls add a few more drops of water to loosen the consistency a little.

Fit one piping bag with a writing tip and fill it with the thick blue icing. Carefully pipe around the star shape to create an outline, then set aside to allow the icing to set for 15 minutes.

Once set, fill a second piping bag with the looser light blue icing and slowly fill the center of the stars with the icing. Set the icing aside and allow it to set for 1 hour.

Lastly, fit a final piping bag with a writing tip and, using the white icing, pipe on the details (you can copy the photo or be as creative as you like) and set aside to harden for another hour before serving.

❧ TIDE POOL COOKIES ❧

A tide pool is a special place filled with hidden treasures. Replicate your own foodie version and uncover the tasty treasure hiding in between two delicious cookies.

Makes: 15 ❧ **Time: 45 minutes** ❧ **Difficulty rating:** ★

INGREDIENTS

- ★ 9 tablespoons butter
- ★ 5 ounces dark chocolate (minimum 70 percent cacao)
- ★ 1 cup superfine sugar
- ★ 3 eggs
- ★ 1 teaspoon vanilla extract
- ★ 2 cups plus 1 teaspoon all-purpose flour
- ★ 1¾ cups plus 2 tablespoons cocoa powder
- ★ ½ teaspoon baking powder
- ★ Tub of ice cream, your choice of color (pistachio is pictured)

EXTRA EQUIPMENT

You will need an electric hand mixer and an ice cream scoop.

METHOD

Preheat the oven to 350°F and line two baking sheets with parchment paper. Set aside.

Melt the butter and chocolate in a heatproof bowl set over a saucepan of simmering water, then whisk the sugar, eggs, and vanilla together in a separate bowl.

Let the chocolate cool a little, then fold the sugar and egg mixture into the chocolate.

Add the flour, cocoa powder, and baking powder to the chocolate mixture and fold in gently.

Spoon the mixture onto the baking sheets to make 30 cookies (one tablespoon of mixture per cookie should suffice), leaving 2 inches between each, and bake in the oven for 6 to 8 minutes.

Remove from the oven and set aside the cookies on a wire cooling rack until cool. Turn half of the cookies over and place a small scoop of your desired ice cream on top of each.

Place a second cookie on top of the ice cream and eat immediately. Repeat with the remaininig cookies and store covered in the freezer.

🐚 OYSTER COOKIES 🐚

Recreate these magical underwater treasures in your very own kitchen.

Makes: 12 🐚 Time: 1 hour 30 minutes 🐚 Difficulty rating: ★ ★

INGREDIENTS

Cookies

* ★ ¾ cup plus 2 tablespoons butter, softened
* ★ ½ cup plus 2 tablespoons confectioners' sugar
* ★ 2 teaspoons vanilla extract
* ★ ½ cup all-purpose flour
* ★ 1 tablespoon cornstarch
* ★ ½ teaspoon baking powder
* ★ ½ teaspoon salt
* ★ 2 tablespoons milk (if needed)

Icing

* ★ ⅔ cup butter, softened
* ★ 2½ cups plus 1 tablespoon confectioners' sugar
* ★ 1 teaspoon vanilla extract
* ★ 1 tablespoon milk (if needed)
* ★ Blue gel food coloring (optional)

Pearls

* ★ 2 tablespoons white fondant icing

EXTRA EQUIPMENT

You will need an electric hand mixer, two piping bags, and a large open-star piping tip.

METHOD

For the cookies:

Preheat the oven to 350°F and line two large baking sheets with parchment paper. Set aside.

Beat the butter and sugar together in a large bowl with an electric hand mixer. When the mixture is pale in color, add the vanilla extract and beat again.

Sift the flour, cornstarch, baking powder, and salt into the bowl and fold it into the mixture to combine. If the dough is very stiff at this stage, add the milk, half a teaspoon at a time, until it is smoother. The dough should be smooth, slightly sticky to the touch, and hold its shape.

Fit a piping bag with a large open-star tip and fill it with the cookie dough.

Pipe the cookie rounds onto your parchment paper in a swirl shape (pipe from the center outward). Keep the rounds roughly 1 inch apart.

Bake the cookies for 10 to 12 minutes, or until they are golden around the edges. When done, allow them to cool on the tray before transferring them to a cooling rack.

For the icing:

Place the butter and sugar in a large bowl and beat until pale and fluffy.

Add the vanilla extract and beat again.

At this stage, the mixture should be soft enough to run a spoon through but strong enough to hold its shape. If the mixture is too stiff, add milk a drop at a time to loosen it.

Add a drop of blue gel food coloring and mix until it is well incorporated. Keep adding more color by degrees until you reach the shade you want.

Cover the bowl with plastic wrap and set aside until you're ready to assemble the cookies.

For the pearls:

Take ½ teaspoon of fondant icing and use your hands to roll it into a ball about ½ inch wide. Repeat this twelve times to give you one pearl per oyster cookie.

Assembling the cookies:

Prepare a piping bag with a star-shaped tip and fill it with the buttercream icing.

Take one oyster cookie and pipe a swirl of icing onto the flat side.

Place a pearl at the front of the swirl.

Take a second oyster cookie and place it on top of the swirl, flat side towards the icing. It should be positioned at an angle to look like an open oyster.

🐚 HERMIT CRAB COOKIES 🐚

These are possibly the cutest crabs you'll ever have the pleasure to meet.
Make sure you give them some edible sand (aka brown sugar)
to stand on when serving to create the ultimate beach scene.

Makes: 15 🐚 Time: 2 hours 🐚 Difficulty rating: ⭐

INGREDIENTS

Ginger cookies

- ★ 1⅔ cups all-purpose flour
- ★ ½ teaspoon salt
- ★ 1 teaspoon baking powder
- ★ 1½ teaspoons baking soda
- ★ 2 teaspoons ground ginger
- ★ ⅓ cup plus 2 tablespoons butter
- ★ ⅓ cup plus 2 tablespoons confectioners' sugar
- ★ ¼ cup corn syrup
- ★ 1 tablespoon milk

Decorations

- ★ 6½ tablespoons cream cheese
- ★ Red gel food coloring
- ★ 15 strawberries
- ★ 30 edible eyes
- ★ Soft brown sugar

EXTRA EQUIPMENT

You will need a 2½-inch circle cutter, a piping bag, and a round piping tip.

METHOD

For the ginger cookies:

Preheat the oven to 350°F and line two baking sheets with parchment paper. Set aside.

Combine the flour, salt, baking powder, baking soda, and ground ginger in a large bowl, then add the butter and rub the mixture together with your fingers to form what resembles breadcrumbs. Stir in the sugar.

In a separate bowl, mix the corn syrup and milk until the corn syrup dissolves. Stir this liquid into the breadcrumb mixture, then bring it all together with your hands to form a dough.

Break off small bits of dough and roll them into small balls roughly 1 tablespoon in size. Space 6 to 8 balls out onto each baking sheet, ensuring you leave enough room for them to spread during baking.

Bake for 10 minutes, until golden brown, but keep your eyes on them toward the end of baking, as they can darken very quickly.

Once out of the oven, leave them on the sheets for a few minutes to firm up, then transfer to a wire rack to fully cool.

For the decorations:

In a small bowl, combine the cream cheese with a small drop of red gel food coloring.

Fit a piping bag with a round piping tip, transfer the cream cheese to the bag, and pipe rounds onto each cookie.

Cut off the tops of the strawberries to remove the stalks and use the remains of the tops to cut out small slices for the crab claws.

Assemble the crabs by placing the strawberries on top of the cream cheese rounds and placing two eyes underneath.

Stick the strawberry claws to the cream cheese, on either side of the eyes.

For added effect, sprinkle some soft brown sugar on top of the strawberries so it looks like the crabs just dug themselves out of the sand.

BARS AND BITES

❀ PEBBLE PRETZEL BITES ❀

Who would have thought pebbles could be so yummy and soft?

Makes: 60 ❀ Time: 2 hours ❀ Difficulty rating: ★ ★

INGREDIENTS

Pretzels

- ★ 5 tablespoons light brown sugar
- ★ 2 cups warm water (104°F)
- ★ 5½ teaspoons active dry yeast
- ★ ¼ cup vegetable oil
- ★ 6¼ cups all-purpose flour, divided
- ★ 7 tablespoons baking soda
- ★ 8½ cups water
- ★ 1 egg, beaten

Cinnamon sugar coating

- ★ ⅓ cup plus 2 tablespoons superfine sugar
- ★ 2 tablespoons ground cinnamon
- ★ 2 tablespoons butter

METHOD

For the pretzels:

Grease a large bowl with oil and set aside.

In another large bowl, place the brown sugar and warm water, and stir until the sugar dissolves.

Sprinkle the yeast over the water and let it stand for about 5 minutes, until foamy.

Stir in the vegetable oil and 3¾ cups of the flour until combined, then turn the dough out onto a floured surface and knead in the remaining 2½ cups flour. The dough will be slightly sticky, but continue kneading for around 3 minutes, until smooth and silky. If the dough is very sticky, add flour a tablespoon at a time until it's smooth.

Transfer the dough to the large greased bowl and cover it with plastic wrap, then let it stand somewhere warm for about 1 hour, until it has doubled in size.

Meanwhile, preheat the oven to 475°F and line three large baking sheets with parchment paper. Set aside.

When the dough has doubled in size, punch it down to release all the air and turn it out onto a floured surface. Knead the dough lightly, then cut it into six equal rectangles.

Roll each section into rope-like shapes around 15 inches long, then cut each section into about ten 1½-inch pieces. Let sit uncovered on the lined baking sheets for 10 minutes.

To cook your pretzels, place 8½ cups of water in a large saucepan with 7 tablespoons of baking soda and bring to a simmer over high heat.

Lower the heat to medium and, using two forks, carefully transfer six pretzel bites at a time to the simmering water and leave them for 30 seconds. Transfer each bite to a paper towel to drain, then return to the baking sheets, spacing them evenly apart.

Continue this process with the remaining bites.

Create an egg wash by cracking the egg into a bowl and whisking it together with a tablespoon of water, then brush each pretzel bite with the egg wash.

Bake in the oven for about 10 minutes, until dark brown.

For the cinnamon sugar coating:

Combine the superfine sugar and cinnamon together in a bowl and set aside.

Melt the butter gently in a pan and dip each baked pretzel bite into the butter and then into the cinnamon sugar mixture until fully coated.

Serve warm or at room temperature.

✿ MERMAID KISSES ✿

One kiss from a mermaid gives you gills and the ability to breathe underwater. If you haven't had the good fortune of receiving a kiss from a mermaid, these vibrant peaks of meringue are almost as exciting.

Makes: 24 to 30 ✿ **Time: 1 hour 30 minutes** ✿ **Difficulty rating:** ★ ★ ★

INGREDIENTS

- ★ ⅓ cup superfine sugar
- ★ ⅔ cup confectioners' sugar
- ★ 3 egg whites
- ★ Turquoise and purple gel food coloring

EXTRA EQUIPMENT

You will need an electric hand mixer, a piping bag, a round piping tip, and a clean cake-decorating paintbrush.

METHOD

Preheat the oven to 250°F and line two large baking sheets with parchment paper. Set aside.

In a small bowl, mix both of the sugars together and set aside.

In a clean bowl, beat the egg whites on medium speed for 2 minutes until they form stiff peaks.

Begin adding the sugar a tablespoon at a time, beating for 30 seconds between each tablespoon. Continue until you have used all the sugar and have a glossy meringue that holds stiff peaks.

Turn a piping bag inside out and, using a paintbrush, paint two lines of the turquoise gel food coloring, followed by two lines of purple gel food coloring, from the top to almost the end of the bag. Turn the piping bag back the right way so the painted lines are on the inside, and fit it with a round piping tip.

Fill with a few tablespoons of the meringue mix and twist the end to close. Holding the bag at a 90-degree angle over one of the lined sheets, apply pressure at the start, then quickly draw the bag upwards to create little points. The painted-on color will give the meringues a striped pattern as they pass through the bag.

Pipe out around 12 to 15 meringue kisses on each baking tray, then bake in the oven for 1 hour, or until they sound hollow when tapped.

Turn off the oven and slowly let cool. Store in an airtight container until ready to use.

These will keep in an airtight container for 7 to 10 days.

❧ MERMAID ENERGY BALLS ❧

These energy balls are perfect healthy snacks for times when you need to recharge your energy levels and give yourself a little mermaid strength.

Makes: 12 ❧ Time: 1 hour 30 minutes ❧ Difficulty rating: ★

INGREDIENTS

* ★ 24 apricots
* ★ 4 dates, soaked
* ★ ⅓ cup plus 1 tablespoon desiccated coconut
* ★ ⅓ cup plus 1 tablespoon shredded coconut
* ★ ½ cup sliced almonds
* ★ 2 tablespoons honey
* ★ 1 teaspoon vanilla extract

EXTRA EQUIPMENT

You will need a food processor.

METHOD

Line a baking sheet with parchment paper. Set aside.

Place all the ingredients in a food processor and pulse for 1 minute, until the mixture comes together.

Take a teaspoon of the mixture and roll it between your palms to form a ball. Place it on the baking sheet and repeat until you have used all the mixture.

Eat immediately or leave in the fridge for 20 minutes.

Keep refrigerated in an airtight container for 7 days or freeze in a freezer bag or container for up to 3 months.

❧ STORMY SEA BROWNIES ❧

It is often said that mermaids surface during storms to calm the seas and save those in danger. Bake up a storm with these brownies and watch all your fellow mermaids gather 'round to save you from eating the whole batch.

Makes: 16 ❧ Time: 1 hour ❧ Difficulty rating: ★ ★

INGREDIENTS

Brownie batter

* ★ 4 ounces dark chocolate (minimum 70 percent cacao)
* ★ 4 ounces milk chocolate
* ★ ⅔ cup butter
* ★ 3 eggs
* ★ 1 cup superfine sugar
* ★ ¾ cup plus 1 tablespoon all-purpose flour

Cheesecake mixture

* ★ 1 cup plus 2 tablespoons cream cheese
* ★ ¼ cup superfine sugar
* ★ 1 egg yolk
* ★ ¼ teaspoon peppermint extract
* ★ Turquoise gel food coloring

EXTRA EQUIPMENT

You will need an 8-inch square baking pan.

METHOD

For the brownie batter:

Preheat the oven to 325°F, and grease and line an 8-inch square baking pan. Set aside.

Melt the chocolate and butter in a heatproof bowl set over a saucepan of simmering water. Once the ingredients have melted, remove the bowl from the pan and set aside to cool slightly.

While the mixture cools, whisk the eggs and superfine sugar in a large bowl until well combined. Add the eggs and sugar to the melted chocolate and butter, and whisk together for 1 minute.

Add the flour and, using a metal spoon, carefully fold it into the mixture until fully incorporated.

For the cheesecake mixture:

Beat the cream cheese, superfine sugar, egg yolk, and peppermint extract together until smooth.

Add a tiny drop of the turquoise gel food coloring and mix it in to create a mint color.

Pour the brownie batter into the brownie pan, smoothing it out into all corners, then spoon the mint cheesecake mixture in a random formation on top. Using the tip of a knife, swirl the two mixtures together to create a marbled effect.

Bake in the oven for 25 to 30 minutes. Remove from the oven, leave in the pan, and set aside to cool completely before peeling off the parchment paper and cutting into equal squares.

🐚 MERMAZING FUDGE 🐚

Be mesmerized by the swirls and the taste of this indulgent white chocolate fudge.

Makes: 30 🐚 **Time: 1 hour 15 minutes** 🐚 **Difficulty rating:** ⭐

INGREDIENTS

* ★ 14½ ounces good quality white chocolate, broken into pieces
* ★ 1 (14 ounce) can sweetened condensed milk
* ★ 2 tablespoons butter
* ★ ¾ cup plus 2 tablespoons confectioners' sugar
* ★ Turquoise gel food coloring
* ★ Edible pearl sprinkles

EXTRA EQUIPMENT

You will need an 8-inch square baking pan.

METHOD

Line an 8-inch square pan with parchment paper. Set aside.

Place the chocolate in a non-stick saucepan, then add the sweetened condensed milk and butter. Melt the ingredients gently over low heat, stirring occasionally until smooth.

Sift in the confectioners' sugar and mix thoroughly to remove any lumps, then pour the mixture into the lined pan and smooth over.

Add a few drops of turquoise gel food coloring and swirl it around the fudge mixture with a toothpick to create a marbled effect.

Decorate with pearl sprinkles and chill in the fridge for 1 hour until set.

To serve, cut it into squares and store in an airtight container in the fridge for up to 2 weeks.

🐚 FISH DOUGHNUTS 🐚

Transform plain old ring doughnuts into a school of multi-colored fish with this recipe.

Makes: 8   🐚   Time: 2 hours   🐚   Difficulty rating: ⭐ ⭐ ⭐

INGREDIENTS

Doughnuts

- ★ 2½ cups bread flour, plus extra for dusting when kneading
- ★ 2 tablespoons superfine sugar
- ★ ⅓ cup butter, softened
- ★ 2 eggs
- ★ 2 teaspoons instant yeast
- ★ 1 teaspoon salt
- ★ ⅓ cup warm milk
- ★ 4 tablespoons water, divided
- ★ 4¼ cups sunflower oil, for frying

Decorations

- ★ 1¾ cups confectioners' sugar
- ★ 5 teaspoons cold water
- ★ Candy-coated chocolate pieces
- ★ 8 edible eyes

EXTRA EQUIPMENT

You will need a 3-inch circle cutter and a 1-inch circle cutter.

METHOD

For the doughnuts:

Place all the ingredients, except the sunflower oil, into a large bowl, then add 3 tablespoons of the water and stir with your hands to make a dough. Gradually add another tablespoon of water and knead it in.

Turn the dough out onto a lightly floured surface and knead well for 10 minutes, or until the dough becomes smooth and elastic.

Place the dough in a bowl, cover with a damp tea towel, and let rise somewhere warm for 40 minutes.

When it has doubled in size, turn the dough out again onto a very lightly floured surface and divide it in half.

With a floured rolling pin, roll out the dough to about ½ inch thick and cut out 8 circles using the 3-inch circle cutter. Using the 1-inch cutter, cut smaller circles out of the middle of each 2-inch circle.

Spin each doughnut on your index finger to expand the hole a little.

Place the doughnuts on an oiled baking sheet, loosely cover with plastic wrap, and let rise for 30 minutes.

Frying the doughnuts:

(Safety note: cooking with hot oil can be dangerous and safety instructions should be followed to avoid accidents. Before frying, ensure young children are kept away from the frying pan and you are

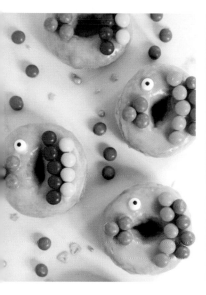  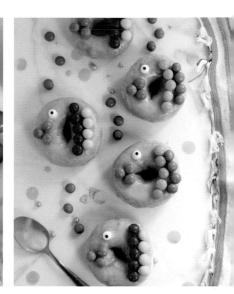

protected by wearing long sleeves. Never leave oil heating on a stove unattended. Use a large, sturdy frying pan and keep the pan's handles away from the front of the stove to avoid knocking it off the burner. While frying, keep your eyes away from the pan in case the oil pops at you. Have a large slotted spoon ready to lift out the doughnuts.)

Prepare two baking sheets with parchment paper and place them near where you will be frying your doughnuts. Fill a large, deep frying pan with sunflower oil and heat to 350°F.

Carefully drop the doughnuts in one at a time, cooking each side for about 1 minute, or until golden-brown. Remove with a slotted spoon, place onto the lined baking sheet, and let cool.

For the decorations:

Place the confectioners' sugar in a large bowl and gradually add the cold water, mixing it to create a thick paste.

When the doughnuts have cooled, dip the tops of them into the icing. Let set slightly for 5 minutes.

When the icing is still a little sticky, create the scales by placing five of the same colored chocolate pieces on one half of the doughnut, surrounding the ring. Then add four different colored chocolate pieces next to the first row. To create the face, add an edible eye and three chocolate pieces that are a third color in a triangle shape.

Let set on a cooling rack before serving, and eat within 24 hours.

❀ SEAWEED COCONUT BARS ❀

One bite of these coconut bars and you will take your taste buds on an underwater adventure.

Makes: 12   ❀   Time: 2 hours   ❀   Difficulty rating: ★

INGREDIENTS

* 1⅔ cups desiccated coconut
* 1 (14 ounce) can sweetened condensed milk
* Pinch of salt
* Blue gel food coloring
* 3½ ounces dark chocolate (minimum 70 percent cacao)
* 7 ounces milk chocolate
* Edible silver and turquoise glitter

EXTRA EQUIPMENT

You will need a 9 by 13-inch baking sheet.

METHOD

Line a baking sheet with parchment paper. Set aside.

In a large bowl, mix the desiccated coconut, condensed milk, salt, and blue gel food coloring until well combined.

Fill the baking sheet with the mixture and smooth it out, packing it down as you go. Put in the freezer to set hard for around 1 hour.

Once set, cut it into equal 4 by 1-inch rectangles and pop back into the freezer while you melt the chocolate.

Set a heatproof bowl over a saucepan of simmering water and melt the dark and milk chocolate together. Let the chocolate cool slightly, then remove the coconut bars from the freezer and dip each one into the chocolate using two forks. Place the coated bars back on the lined baking sheet and sprinkle with the edible glitter.

Leave on a baking sheet and let the chocolate set for 30 minutes before transferring to the fridge or somewhere cold for 1 hour. These will keep for 3 days if stored somewhere cool in an airtight container.

❀ MAGICAL MERMAID ROCKS ❀

Adorned with edible pearls and a shimmer of glitter,
these Magical Mermaid Rocks will be a hit at any party.

Makes: 1 baking sheet ❀ **Time: 1 hour 15 minutes** ❀ **Difficulty rating:** ★

INGREDIENTS

* ★ 14 ounces white chocolate
* ★ Pink and turquoise gel food coloring
* ★ Edible pearl sprinkles
* ★ Edible silver glitter

EXTRA EQUIPMENT

You will need a toothpick and a mermaid tail mold (optional).

METHOD

Line a baking sheet with parchment paper and set aside.

Place the white chocolate in a heatproof bowl over a saucepan of simmering water and, stirring occasionally, let it melt down completely.

Remove from the heat and split the white chocolate equally between three bowls.

Add ¼ teaspoon pink gel food coloring to one bowl, ¼ teaspoon turquoise gel food coloring to another, and leave the last bowl plain.

Fill the mermaid mold with a small amount from each of the bowls of chocolate and swirl them together gently, then leave in the freezer to set hard for 5 minutes. Carefully remove the mermaid tail from the mold and set aside. For the second mermaid tail, fill the mold again and freeze for another 5 minutes until set.

Place spoonfuls of each mixture in a random formation onto the parchment paper, then swirl the mixture together gently with a toothpick. Add the set chocolate mermaid tails, then scatter sprinkles and edible glitter over the top.

Let the chocolate set at room temperature for 45 minutes, then place it in the fridge for 15 minutes to set hard before breaking it into shards.

Mermaid rocks are a great gift and can be wrapped in cellophane and given for a special occasion. If you're keeping them for yourself, the shards are best stored in an airtight container and kept in the fridge or at room temperature for up to 5 days—if you can make them last that long.

PARTY
FOOD

🐚 PEARL OF THE OCEAN MACARONS 🐚

Pearls are expensive and much sought-after gems—now you can feel like royalty as you taste one of the ocean's treasures with these pearl macarons.

Makes: 12 🐚 Time: 2 hours 🐚 Difficulty rating: ★★★

INGREDIENTS

Macaron shells

* ⅔ cup almond meal
* 1¼ cups confectioners' sugar
* 2 large egg whites, room temperature
* Purple gel food coloring
* ¼ cup superfine sugar

Buttercream filling

* ⅓ cup plus 1 tablespoon butter, softened
* 1¾ cups confectioners' sugar
* 1 teaspoon vanilla extract
* Pinch of sea salt
* 12 edible cream pearls

EXTRA EQUIPMENT

You will need a stand mixer or electric hand mixer, two piping bags, a small round piping tip, and a small open-star piping tip. To decorate, you will need a fine-tipped paintbrush.

METHOD

For the macaron shells:

Preheat the oven to 300°F and line two baking sheets with parchment paper. Set aside.

Place the almond meal and confectioners' sugar in a standing mixer, or use a hand mixer, and beat for about 1 minute, then transfer to a mixing bowl.

Beat one of the egg whites into the almond and confectioners' sugar mixture to make a smooth paste. Add a few drops purple gel food coloring and mix to fully combine, then cover the bowl with a tea towel.

Pour the second egg white into a super-clean bowl and begin to beat on high speed to form peaks. Gradually add the superfine sugar 1 tablespoon at a time, until it starts to stiffen. Once all the sugar has been added, continue beating on a high setting for 2 minutes, until the mixture resembles stiff, glossy peaks.

Add the egg white mixture to the almond paste and, using a spatula, fold the two together from the bottom up. Continue that motion 15 to 20 times, until the mixture is fully incorporated and flows like molten lava.

Transfer the mixture into a piping bag fitted with a small round tip and pipe 24 shell shapes onto the two lined baking sheets. The mixture will spread, so pipe to around 50 percent of the size you want.

Tap the sheets on a work surface a few times to release any air bubbles, then let them dry for 30 minutes. They will be ready to bake when they are no longer sticky or wet when touched.

Bake on the middle rack of the oven for 8 minutes. Open the oven to let out any steam and turn the sheets around, then bake for a further 8 minutes, until the tops are crisp.

Let them cool fully before removing from the baking sheet.

Once fully cooled, decorate the shells by mixing ¼ teaspoon of the purple gel food coloring with a tiny drop of water to help thin the food coloring. Paint thin lines down the shells to replicate the ridges.

For the buttercream:
Cream together the butter and confectioners' sugar until smooth and fluffy.

Add the vanilla extract and sea salt and mix to combine.

Transfer to a piping bag fitted with a small open-star tip and pipe the buttercream onto one half of the macaron shells. Rest an edible pearl on the buttercream toward the front of the macarons and top with the remaining macaron shells. Leave in the fridge for 30 minutes before serving.

These will store in an airtight container for a few days if kept in the fridge.

🐚 CORAL REEF ÉCLAIRS 🐚

These colorful delights will transport you to an underwater world teeming with friendly fish and vibrant reefs.

Makes: 8 🐚 **Time: 1 hour** 🐚 **Difficulty rating:** ⭐ ⭐

INGREDIENTS

Choux pastry

- ★ ½ cup water
- ★ ¼ cup butter, chilled
- ★ ½ cup plus 1 tablespoon all-purpose flour, sifted
- ★ Pinch of salt
- ★ 2 eggs, lightly beaten

Filling and topping

- ★ ¾ cup whipping cream
- ★ 1 teaspoon vanilla extract
- ★ 3½ cups confectioners' sugar, divided
- ★ 7 ounces white chocolate, broken into squares
- ★ ¾ cup plus 2 tablespoons butter, softened
- ★ Gel food coloring (pink, orange, and green)

EXTRA EQUIPMENT

You will need five piping bags, a ½-inch round tip, three closed-star tips, and a skewer.

METHOD

For the choux pastry:

Preheat the oven to 400°F and line a baking sheet with parchment paper. Set aside.

Place the water and butter in a saucepan over low heat and cook until the butter melts. Increase the heat to medium-high and bring the mixture to a boil.

Remove the pan from the heat and use a wooden spoon to beat in the flour and salt until well combined. Place the pan over a low heat and continue cooking, stirring constantly for 30 seconds, or until the mixture comes away from the sides of the pan.

Set aside for 5 minutes to cool a little, then gradually beat in half the beaten egg. Repeat with the remaining egg, beating until the mixture is thick and glossy.

Transfer the dough mixture to a piping bag fitted with a ½-inch round tip. Pipe ten 5-inch long lines onto the lined sheet and bake in the oven for 20 to 25 minutes, or until the éclairs are puffed and golden.

Make a hole in one end of the éclair using a skewer, then bake in the oven for a further 5 minutes. Transfer to a wire rack to cool completely.

For the filling and topping:

Whip the cream with 1 teaspoon of vanilla extract and 5 tablespoons of confectioners' sugar in a bowl until stiff.

Fill a piping bag fitted with a small round tip and pipe in the whipped cream through the hole you created at one end of the éclair.

For the white chocolate glaze, melt the chocolate in a heatproof bowl set over a pan of simmering water. Once the chocolate has melted, dip the tops of the éclairs in the chocolate and let the chocolate set.

To make the buttercream, mix the butter and the rest of the confectioners' sugar together until combined and fluffy. Split the mixture between three bowls and add a few drops of gel food coloring to each (so one bowl is pink, one orange, and one green). Fill three piping bags with the different colored buttercream and fit them with the closed-star tips. Pipe random peaks of the buttercream on top of the éclairs, then serve.

Store in an airtight container in the refrigerator for up to 3 days.

🐚 SHARK TEETH KEBABS 🐚

These kebabs certainly don't bite, but they do pack a punch.

Makes: 4 🐚 **Time: 30 minutes** 🐚 **Difficulty rating:** ⭐

INGREDIENTS

* ½ of a watermelon
* 4 kiwi fruits
* 8 to 10 strawberries, hulled
* 16 to 18 blueberries

EXTRA EQUIPMENT

You will need four wooden kebab skewers.

METHOD

Slice the watermelon into 1-inch thick slices and remove the flesh from the skin.

Cut out four 2-inch square cubes from the watermelon, then cut them diagonally in half to create triangles and set aside.

Peel and thickly slice the kiwi fruits into eight pieces, then cut them into triangle shapes and set aside.

Slice the strawberries in half lengthwise and set aside.

Assemble by piercing a piece of watermelon, followed by two blueberries, then a strawberry, then a kiwi fruit onto a kebab skewer.

Repeat this step to fill the kebab skewer.

Continue with the remaining skewers and serve the fruit kebabs on their own or with a bowl of melted chocolate for dipping.

⚜ MERMAID MARSHMALLOW ⚜ CRISPY BARS

Get nostalgic with these crispy bars, which are made from all your favorite childhood indulgences.

Makes: 8 ⚜ **Time: 1 hour 30 minutes** ⚜ **Difficulty rating:** ☆

INGREDIENTS

* ★ ¼ cup butter
* ★ 4½ cups mini marshmallows
* ★ 5 cups puffed rice
* ★ 7 ounces white chocolate
* ★ Turquoise gel food coloring
* ★ Edible flower cupcake toppers
* ★ Edible pearl sprinkles
* ★ Edible glitter

EXTRA EQUIPMENT

You will need an 8-inch square baking pan.

METHOD

Grease the baking pan and set aside.

Place the butter and marshmallows in a large saucepan and melt together on the stove over medium heat.

Once melted, add the puffed rice and mix together until well coated.

Transfer the sticky mixture into the greased baking pan, spread it out into all corners, and flatten the top. Allow to set for 1 hour at room temperature.

Once set, flip the baking pan upside down and tap the bottom until the mixture falls out, then cut it into eight equal squares.

To decorate, melt the white chocolate in a heatproof bowl set over a saucepan of simmering water. Add a drop of turquoise gel food coloring and stir until you have a mint green color. Let cool for 5 minutes.

Dip the marshmallow squares halfway into the chocolate and lay them out on a baking sheet lined with parchment paper. Allow to set in the fridge for 10 minutes, then repeat for a second coat.

Top with edible pearl sprinkles and a dusting of edible glitter, then, with a little remaining white chocolate, stick the sugar flowers above the dipped white chocolate to resemble a mermaid bikini.

🐚 PEARL CAKE POPS 🐚

Smooth and silky, these cake pops reflect what pearls would taste like if they were edible.

Makes: 20 🐚 **Time: 1 to 2 hours** 🐚 **Difficulty rating:** ⭐

INGREDIENTS

Cake
* ½ cup butter, softened
* ⅔ cup superfine sugar
* 1½ cups plus 1 tablespoon self-rising flour
* 4 tablespoons milk
* 2 eggs
* 1 teaspoon vanilla extract

Frosting
* ⅓ cup butter, softened
* 1 teaspoon vanilla extract
* 3 tablespoons cream cheese, softened
* 1¾ cups confectioners' sugar, sifted

Decorations
* 17½ ounces melted white chocolate
* 1 teaspoon vegetable oil
* Blue and green gel food coloring
* ¾ cup plus 2 tablespoons sugar
* Edible silver glitter

EXTRA EQUIPMENT

You will need an electric hand mixer, an 8-inch cake pan, 20 lollipop sticks, and a cake-pop stand.

METHOD

For the cake:

Preheat the oven to 350°F and line an 8-inch cake pan and a baking sheet with parchment paper. Set aside.

Place the butter, sugar, flour, milk, eggs, and vanilla into a bowl and beat together for 2 to 3 minutes, until smooth, pale, and fluffy.

Pour the mixture into the prepared pan, bake for 35 to 40 minutes, and let the cake cool on a wire rack.

For the frosting:

Cream the butter, vanilla, and cream cheese together until smooth and gradually add the confectioners' sugar, then continue to mix until light and fluffy. Refrigerate for 30 minutes.

For the cake pops:

Crumble the cooled cake in a large mixing bowl with your hands until you have fine crumbs.

Add heaped tablespoons of the cream cheese frosting and begin mixing it in with the crumbs. You may not require all the frosting, as it will depend on how moist your cake is. Keep mixing and adding the frosting until you have a fudge-like texture that doesn't crumble when squeezed between your hands.

Wrap the mixture in plastic wrap and chill for at least 1 hour to firm up.

Once chilled, break off small pieces of the mixture (about the size of a ping-pong ball) and roll them into balls with your hands. You want to make 20 balls in total. Place each ball on the lined baking tray and put it in the fridge for 15 to 20 minutes.

For the decorations:

Melt the white chocolate in a heatproof bowl set over a saucepan of simmering water, then mix in 1 teaspoon of vegetable oil. This will make the melted chocolate smoother and easier to coat the cake pops with.

Split the chocolate into two bowls, and add a few drops of the blue gel food coloring to one and a few drops of green gel food coloring to the other. Mix both and, if necessary, add more food coloring until you have a bowl of vibrant blue chocolate and a bowl of vibrant green chocolate.

To assemble the cake pops, dip the lollipop sticks into either the blue or green melted chocolate, one at a time, and then push each of them into the middle of one of the cake pops. (Dipping the sticks into the chocolate first will help secure them to the cake balls.) Then dip the entire surface of the cake pops into your desired chocolate (green or blue) until fully coated, making sure you hold them upside down for a few seconds to let the excess chocolate drip off. Once they are coated with chocolate, place them in the cake-pop stand and sprinkle edible glitter onto half of the blue cake pops. Chill all the cake pops in the fridge or in a cool room for 1 hour.

Meanwhile, mix the confectioners' sugar and a few teaspoons of water in a large bowl until you have a ribbon consistency.

Split the mixture into two bowls, color one bowl blue, and leave the other bright white.

When the cake pops are set, drizzle the white icing over the blue cake pops that aren't covered in edible glitter and leave them upside down on a plate.

Then drizzle blue and white icing over the green cake pops and leave them aside on the plate upside down to set completely before serving.

⚜ OCTOPUS ARM CHURROS ⚜

Did you know that an octopus can regrow its arms? If you end up eating all these churros, be like an octopus and make some more!

Makes: 8 ⚜ **Time: 2 hours** ⚜ **Difficulty rating:** ★ ★

INGREDIENTS

Churros

* 1½ cups boiling water
* ¼ cup butter, melted
* ½ teaspoon vanilla extract
* 2 cups plus 1 tablespoon all-purpose flour
* 1 teaspoon baking powder
* 4¼ cups sunflower oil
* ⅓ cup plus 1 tablespoon superfine sugar
* 2 teaspoons cinnamon

Chocolate sauce

* 7 ounces dark chocolate
* ½ cup heavy cream
* ½ cup whole milk
* 3 tablespoons light corn syrup
* ½ teaspoon vanilla extract

EXTRA EQUIPMENT

You will need a pitcher, a large piping bag, and a 1-inch open-star piping tip.

METHOD

For the churro dough:

Measure 1½ cups boiling water into a pitcher and add the melted butter and vanilla extract.

Sift the flour and baking powder into a large mixing bowl, make a well in the center, and pour in the butter and water mixture, beating it into the flour quickly with a wooden spoon until lump-free. Let stand for 10 to 15 minutes.

For the chocolate sauce:

Place all the sauce ingredients in a saucepan and gently melt them together, stirring until you have a smooth, shiny sauce. Keep warm on a low heat, stirring occasionally.

Frying the churros:

(*Safety note: cooking with hot oil can be dangerous and safety instructions should be followed to avoid accidents. Before frying, ensure young children are kept away from the frying pan and you are protected by wearing long sleeves. Never leave a frying pan of oil heating on a stove unattended. Use a large, sturdy pan and keep the frying pan's handles away from the front of the stove to avoid*

knocking it off the burner. While frying, keep your eyes away from the pan in case the oil pops at you. Have a large slotted spoon or sturdy tongs ready to lift out the churros.)

Prepare two baking sheets by lining one with parchment paper and spreading the superfine sugar and cinnamon on the other, mixing them together to form cinnamon sugar.

Fit a large piping bag with the open-star piping tip, fill it with the dough, then set it aside.

Fill a large, deep frying pan with sunflower oil so that it is no more than two-thirds full.

Heat the oil until it reaches 350°F, then pipe 2 to 3 strips about 4 to 6 inches long directly into the pan, snipping off each dough strip with a pair of kitchen scissors. (***Note: be extra careful when adding the dough to the hot oil.***)

Fry for 45 seconds to 1 minute, until golden brown and crisp, then remove with a slotted spoon or tongs and drain on the lined baking sheet.

Add your next batch of churro strips to the oil, then return to the cooked churros and roll them in the cinnamon sugar.

Continue the process until all churros are cooked and coated, then serve with the chocolate sauce for dipping.

These are best eaten immediately.

🐚 SEABED ROCKY ROAD 🐚

Just like a seabed, this rocky road has lots of hidden gems in it.

Makes: 12 🐚 **Time: 1 hour 30 minutes** 🐚 **Difficulty rating:** ⭐

INGREDIENTS

* ★ 1⅔ cups chocolate graham crackers (or 13½ cracker sheets)
* ★ ½ cup plus 1 tablespoon butter
* ★ 3½ ounces dark chocolate
* ★ 3½ ounces milk chocolate
* ★ 2 to 3 tablespoons corn syrup
* ★ 2½ cups mini marshmallows
* ★ ¼ cup glacé cherries
* ★ Assorted candy (mints, chocolate chips, etc.), for dusting
* ★ Confectioners' sugar, for dusting

EXTRA EQUIPMENT

You will need a square 8-inch baking pan and a freezer bag.

METHOD

Line the baking pan with parchment paper. Set aside.

Place the graham crackers in a freezer bag and crush with a rolling pin until you have a mixture of fine crumbs and larger pieces. Set aside.

In a large pan, melt the butter, chocolate, and corn syrup over medium heat, stirring until completely melted.

Remove the pan from the heat, then add the graham crackers, marshmallows, and glacé cherries and stir it all together until everything is coated.

Pour the mixture into the prepared baking pan, spread it out evenly into all the corners, then top with the assorted candy.

Leave in the fridge for 1 hour to set, then dust with a little confectioners' sugar and cut into 12 equal squares.

⚜ PERSONALIZED MERMAID ⚜ TAIL COOKIES

Did you know that the color of a mermaid's tail depicts her mood and personality? Now you can create your own customized mermaid tail, colored and designed to reflect your very own mermaid personality.

Makes: 15 ⚜ **Time: 2 hours** ⚜ **Difficulty rating:** ★ ★

INGREDIENTS

Cookies

* ⅓ cup plus 1 tablespoon butter, softened
* ⅓ cup plus 2 tablespoons superfine sugar
* 1 egg
* ½ teaspoon vanilla extract
* 1⅔ cups all-purpose flour, plus more for dusting
* ¼ teaspoon salt
* ½ teaspoon baking powder

Icing

* 2 (14 ounce) packages royal icing mix
* ½ cup plus 2 tablespoons cold water
* A variety of gel food colorings

EXTRA EQUIPMENT

You will need a mermaid tail cookie cutter, several piping bags, a writing-tip piping tip, and toothpicks.

METHOD

For the cookies:

Preheat the oven to 350°F and line two baking sheets with parchment paper. Set aside.

Place the butter and sugar in a bowl and cream together with a wooden spoon until smooth, then add the egg and vanilla extract and mix well. Gradually add the flour, salt, and baking powder, and mix to combine into a dough.

On a floured work surface, roll the dough out to a thickness of about ¼ inch, then cut out your mermaid tails with your cutter. You will need to re-roll the leftover dough a few times to be able to cut out all fifteen cookies.

Place the tails on the baking sheets, ensuring they are well spaced out to allow for a little spreading, then bake for 10 to 12 minutes, until light golden brown.

Let cool on a wire rack. If you want to make the cookies ahead of icing them, they will keep for 2 to 3 days in an airtight container stored at room temperature.

  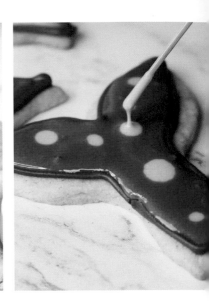

For the different icing techniques:

Pour the cold water into a large bowl and add the royal icing mix.

Combine, slowly at first, to avoid a sugar cloud, then beat for around 5 minutes, until the mixture is bright white and the consistency of toothpaste.

Divide into bowls and color each to your desired shade.

Line icing:

Line icing should be the texture of toothpaste.

To line your cookies, fit a piping bag with a writing tip and fill it with your desired icing color. Pipe around the edges of your mermaid tails, making sure that you join up your trail to form an unbroken wall, and let the walls dry for about 5 minutes.

If you want to add any detail, such as the blue mermaid scales design, set some of your line icing aside so you can pipe this on after you've filled your cookies.

Flood icing:

Flood icing is a runnier consistency and is used to fill in the space between the line icing. To create flood icing, mix a little bit of water into the line icing to create a slightly looser consistency.

Tip: don't add too much at once; take it a few drops at a time to ensure you don't add too much and consequently ruin the icing.

You can pipe the flood icing using a squeeze piping bottle or a piping bag. Just simply fill it with the icing and carefully fill the area you wish to color. Don't add too much, as you can spread it out with a toothpick. If you fill too much, it could overflow the lines.

Let the icing dry for 30 minutes before serving.

Wet on wet:

The polka-dot mermaid tail design was created using the wet-on-wet technique.

To create this, once you have flooded your cookies, simply add a tiny drop of another color straight onto the wet icing, using a toothpick or a piping bag fitted with a writing tip, and watch it merge together.

Marble:

For the marble technique, simply flood the cookies with two or three different colors and mix the colors together with a toothpick to create the marble effect.

Store in a single layer in an airtight container for up to 4 days.

❀ MESMERIZING MADELEINES ❀

Charm your taste buds with these simple, delicious, and light madeleines.

Makes: 12 ❀ **Time: 45 minutes** ❀ **Difficulty rating:** ★

INGREDIENTS

* ⅓ cup plus 2 tablespoons butter, melted (plus a little extra for preparing the tray)
* ¾ cup plus 1 tablespoon all-purpose flour (plus a little extra for preparing the tray)
* 2 eggs
* ⅓ cup plus 2 tablespoons superfine sugar
* Juice and zest of 1 lemon
* ¾ teaspoon baking powder
* Confectioners' sugar, for dusting

EXTRA EQUIPMENT

You will need a madeleine tray and a pastry brush.

METHOD

Preheat the oven to 400°F and brush the madeleine tray with melted butter. Sprinkle in a little flour to coat and tap out any excess. Set aside.

Whisk together the eggs and sugar in a bowl until frothy, then gradually add the butter, lemon juice, and zest, followed by the flour and baking powder, whisking them all in as they are added.

Let stand for 20 minutes before carefully pouring the mixture into the prepared madeleine tray. Bake for 8 to 10 minutes, then transfer to a wire rack and leave for a few minutes to cool slightly. Dust lightly with confectioners' sugar and eat within an hour of baking for the best taste.

🐚 JELLYFISH LAYERED SURPRISE 🐚

*Just before you serve this fruity dessert, salute the jellyfish
that inspired it with a jiggle and a wiggle.*

Serves: 10 to 12 🐚 **Time: 3 hours** 🐚 **Difficulty rating:** ★

INGREDIENTS

* ★ Oil for greasing
* ★ ½ (22-gram) packet strawberry gelatin
* ★ 2½ (12-gram) packets unflavored gelatin powder, divided
* ★ 1 (14-ounce) can sweetened condensed milk
* ★ ½ (22-gram) packet orange gelatin
* ★ 1 (22-gram) packet raspberry gelatin, divided
* ★ 3½ cups boiling water, divided
* ★ 1½ cups cold water, divided

EXTRA EQUIPMENT

You will need a 9 by 5-inch loaf pan and six mixing bowls.

METHOD

Grease a 9 by 5-inch loaf pan with a little oil. Set aside.

In one mixing bowl, add ½ packet of strawberry gelatin to ½ packet of unflavored gelatin powder, then pour in 1 cup of boiling water. Stir until the powder has dissolved. Pour the mixture into the prepared loaf pan and chill in the fridge for 15 to 30 minutes.

Meanwhile, prepare the next layer by stirring together the sweetened condensed milk and ½ cup of boiling water. Set aside.

In a separate bowl, combine ½ cup of cold water and ½ packet of unflavored gelatin powder and allow the mixture to set for 2 to 3 minutes. Once set, pour the gelatin into the sweetened condensed milk and combine. Set aside at room temperature for later.

In a fourth bowl, add ½ packet of unflavored gelatin powder, ½ packet of orange gelatin, and ½ cup of cold water, and let it sit for 5 minutes. Then add ½ cup of boiling water and stir together. Let the mixture cool a little, then add half of the creamy condensed milk mixture and combine to make a light, creamy yellow color. Reserve the other half of condensed milk mixture.

Pour this layer over the set strawberry gelatin and chill in the fridge for 15 to 30 minutes.

For the next layer, add ½ packet of raspberry gelatin with ½ packet of unflavored gelatin powder to a bowl, pour in 1 cup of boiling water, and stir.

Pour mixture on top of the set creamy yellow layer and chill for 15 to 30 minutes.

In another bowl, add ½ packet of unflavored gelatin powder, the remaining ½ packet of raspberry gelatin, and ½ cup of cold water, and let it sit for 5 minutes. Then add ½ cup of boiling water and stir together. Let the mixture cool a little and then add the remaining half of the creamy condensed milk mixture to it, combining to make a light pink color.

Pour this layer over the set raspberry gelatin layer and chill in the fridge for a final 30 minutes.

To serve, cut around the edge of the gelatin to loosen a little, then carefully turn it out onto a serving dish and cut into slices.

BREAKFAST

🐚 MERMAID TOAST 🐚

Start your morning off with a colorful breakfast—it will keep you smiling for the rest of the day!

Serves: 2 🐚 Time: 15 minutes 🐚 Difficulty rating: ⭐

INGREDIENTS

* ½ package (4 ounces) cream cheese, softened
* Pink and turquoise gel food coloring
* 2 slices of white bread
* Handful of raspberries
* 2 or 3 slices of watermelon

EXTRA EQUIPMENT

You will need a ½-inch star cutter.

METHOD

Split the cream cheese between two bowls and add a drop of pink gel food coloring to one bowl and a drop of turquoise gel food coloring to the other to create pastel tones.

Toast two slices of white bread, then let cool slightly.

While the toast cools, cut out four (or more if desired) watermelon stars using a ½-inch star cutter and set aside.

Place half of the pink cream cheese on the top left half of the toast and half of the turquoise cream cheese on the bottom right half.

Using a butter knife, spread the mixture across to cover the toast at a diagonal angle. When the two colors meet, blend them together and then top with the watermelon stars and a few raspberries. Repeat these steps for the second piece of toast.

🐚 STARFISH PANCAKES 🐚

A starfish a day keeps the sea doctor away, so the mermaids say. Whether or not this legend is true, these starfish pancakes will certainly give you a boost of energy.

Makes: 8 🐚 Time: 20 minutes 🐚 Difficulty rating: ★

INGREDIENTS

Grapefruit syrup

* Zest of 2 pink grapefruits
* ⅔ cup superfine sugar
* 1 cup water

Pancakes

* 1¼ cups all-purpose flour
* ½ teaspoon salt
* 1 tablespoon baking powder
* 1 tablespoon superfine sugar
* 1 cup milk
* 1 egg
* 1 teaspoon butter or oil, for frying
* Orange and yellow gel food coloring

Decoration

* Grapefruit slices
* Pomegranate arils

EXTRA EQUIPMENT

You will need one large and one medium-sized star cookie cutter.

METHOD

For the grapefruit syrup:

Wash the grapefruits under cold water and dry before finely zesting the peel until you have one heaping tablespoon. Be careful not to get any of the white pith.

Place the sugar and zest in a bowl and mix, using the back of a wooden spoon, crushing the zest into the sugar until the sugar looks damp. Cover well and let sit for 30 minutes.

Bring the water to a boil in a medium saucepan and stir in the citrus sugar. Simmer the sugar for 3 minutes until it's all dissolved.

Remove from the heat and let it cool a little before straining out the zest and decanting the syrup into a sterilized jar or bottle.

For the pancakes:

Preheat the oven to 200°F. Sift together the flour, salt, and baking powder in a large bowl, and add the superfine sugar. Make a well in the center, pour in the milk, then add the egg and whisk until the pancake batter is smooth.

Divide the mixture between two bowls and add ¼ teaspoon of orange gel food coloring to one and ¼ teaspoon of yellow gel food coloring to the other, mixing to combine.

Pour the orange mixture into a measuring cup and heat a large griddle over medium heat.

Place a small amount of butter in the pan, let it melt, then pour in two circles of pancake batter large enough to cut star shapes out of.

Cook each pancake until bubbles appear on the surface, then flip them over with a spatula and cook for 20 to 30 seconds on the reverse side. You don't want to brown them too much or you'll lose the color.

Set aside the cooked pancakes on a plate and keep in warm oven, then repeat with two more rounds of the orange pancake batter. Once all the orange pancakes are cooked, begin frying the yellow pancake batter.

When all the pancakes are cooked, use a large star-shaped cookie cutter to cut out star shapes from the orange pancake batter. Use the medium star-shaped cookie cutter for the yellow pancakes.

Serve warm with a dash of grapefruit syrup, a slice of fresh grapefruit, and pomegranate arils.

❀ TROPICAL SEA SMOOTHIE BOWL ❀

Plunge into the tropical seas with this delicious coconut and banana bowl.

Serves: 2 ❀ Time: 15 minutes ❀ Difficulty rating: ★

INGREDIENTS

Decorations

- ★ ½ of a papaya
- ★ 2 kiwi fruits
- ★ 2 tablespoons shredded coconut
- ★ Handful of blueberries
- ★ Lemon juice

Smoothie mixture

- ★ 4 bananas
- ★ ¾ cup coconut milk
- ★ ¼ teaspoon spirulina powder
- ★ Handful of ice

EXTRA EQUIPMENT

You will need a blender, a ½-inch star cutter, and a 1-inch flower cutter.

METHOD

For the decorations:

Using the star cutter, cut the papaya into ten star shapes and set aside. Then cut the kiwi fruit into ten flower shapes. Squeeze a little bit of lemon juice over the fruit to keep it fresh and set aside.

For the smoothie mixture:

Place the bananas, coconut milk, spirulina powder, and ice in a blender and blend until smooth. It will take a few pulses to break down the ice.

Split the mixture between two bowls, then lay the kiwi fruit flowers out in a row on one side, followed by the papaya stars, the shredded coconut, and finally the blueberries.

🐚 TURTLE WAFFLES 🐚

These waffles will help you to be more turtle: cool, calm, and collected, Duuuuude.

Makes: 6 🐚 Time: 1 hour 30 minutes 🐚 Difficulty rating: ★

INGREDIENTS

Waffles

* ½ cup milk
* 1 teaspoon active dry yeast
* 1 teaspoon light brown sugar, or more to taste
* 1 cup all-purpose flour
* 1 teaspoon cornstarch
* ¼ teaspoon salt
* ½ cup buttermilk
* 2 tablespoons butter, melted
* 1 small egg, beaten
* Oil to grease

Decorations

* 6 bananas (1 per waffle)
* 1 (6 ounce) package blueberries
* Honey, maple syrup, or chocolate to drizzle
* 12 edible eyes

EXTRA EQUIPMENT

You will need an electric circular waffle maker.

METHOD

For the waffles:

Warm the milk in a small saucepan on low heat until warm enough to hold your finger in, then remove from the heat and stir in the yeast and a pinch of sugar, and let set for 5 minutes or so, until the surface is covered with tiny bubbles.

Meanwhile, whisk together the remaining sugar, flour, cornstarch, and salt in a large bowl and set aside. Then, in a separate bowl, beat together the buttermilk, melted butter, and egg.

Whisk the yeast and milk mixture together, then slowly pour this into the bowl of dry ingredients, mixing gently with a large spoon. Cover loosely with plastic wrap and let sit at room temperature for an hour.

Preheat the oven to 200°F to help keep the waffles you cook warm. Lightly grease then heat your waffle maker.

Pour just enough batter into your waffle maker to cover the base, spreading it out with a metal spatula or knife, then turn down the heat slightly and close the lid. Cook for about 4 minutes, according to the manufacturer's instructions, until golden and crisp. Repeat this process until you have cooked all six waffles.

For the decorations:

For each waffle, peel a banana and cut off one end for the turtle head, then position two edible eyes at the tip.

Cut off the other end of the banana, leaving the midsection about 1 inch long. Take the end section of the banana and cut it in half lengthwise. Then cut the flat end of each half at a slight angle and position one on either side of the waffle for the flippers, with the banana tips pointing out.

Then take the 1-inch midsection, cut it in half, and shape each piece into a slight point. Position one on each side at the bottom of the waffle for the turtle feet.

Decorate with blueberries and a splash of honey, maple syrup, or chocolate, and eat immediately while still warm.

DESSERTS

🐚 MERMAID CHEESECAKE 🐚

Give an ordinary ginger and lime cheesecake a mystical mermaid twist with this beautiful jelly topping.

Serves: 10 🐚 **Time: 5 hours (in stages)** 🐚 **Difficulty rating:** ★ ★ ★

INGREDIENTS

Crust
* 1¼ cups graham crackers (or 10 cracker sheets)
* 3½ ounces ginger snaps (or 18 cookies)
* ⅓ cup plus 2 tablespoons butter, melted

Cheesecake filling
* 1¼ cups plus 2 tablespoons cream cheese, full fat
* 1 (8 ounce) tube mascarpone
* ¾ cup plus 2 tablespoons confectioners' sugar
* Juice and zest of 1 lime
* 2 drops vanilla extract
* 1 cup heavy whipping cream

Scales
* ¾ cup plus 2 tablespoons white fondant icing
* Blue and green gel food coloring

Gelatin topping
* 1 cup plus 2½ tablespoons water
* 1 packet (2½ teaspoons) unflavored gelatin powder
* 1 tablespoon sugar
* Blue and green gel food coloring

EXTRA EQUIPMENT

You will need an 8-inch springform pan, a 1-inch circular cutter (or a large bottle top), and a toothpick (optional).

METHOD

For the crust:

Grease your pan lightly with butter and line the base (but not the sides) with a circle of parchment paper. Lightly grease the parchment, then set aside.

Place the graham crackers and ginger snaps in a large resealable food bag and crush them into fine crumbs with a rolling pin.

Place the crumbs in a bowl. Melt the butter, add this to the crumbs, and stir thoroughly so that the crumbs are evenly coated. Pour the mixture into the pan and press down firmly with the back of a spoon to form an even layer. Be sure to push the mixture to the edges so that there are no gaps. Chill in the fridge for at least 1 hour.

For the cheesecake filling:

Place the cream cheese, mascarpone, confectioners' sugar, lime juice, lime zest, and vanilla extract in a large bowl and beat with an electric hand mixer until smooth.

In a smaller bowl, whip the heavy cream by hand with a whisk or fork until it is thick and smooth. It should hold soft peaks when you lift the whisk from the bowl. Add it to the cream cheese mixture and stir until completely combined.

Take the crust from the fridge. Spoon the cheesecake mixture over the crust and smooth it into an even layer with the back of a teaspoon. Ensure that you push the mixture into the edges so that you don't have any air bubbles. Let set in the fridge for 4 hours or overnight.

For the scales:

Divide the fondant into five equal portions of 3 tablespoons each. Take the first portion of fondant and add one small drop each of blue and green gel food coloring. Fold the fondant to mix the color in. Set aside once you have achieved a pale green-blue color.

Do this for the remaining portions of fondant, adding slightly more color each time so that each portion is slightly darker than the last.

Dust a clean surface with confectioners' sugar. Roll out one of the fondant portions until it is no more than ⅛-inch thick (the thinner you can get it, the better). Cut out circles with the cutter and put them to one side. Re-roll the extra fondant as many times as you need.

To make the scale shape, use the same cutter you used to cut out the circle. Cut out the top left and right quarters of the circle with the edge of the cutter. To keep your scales consistent, you could draw out a template on parchment paper for this step. You may also need to cut off the very tip of the scale for the scales to fit together evenly.

Draw a circle the same size as your cheesecake on a sheet of parchment paper and lay out the scales from light to dark as they will appear on the cheesecake. You will have to cut some so that they fit around the edges. Then leave them uncovered for 3 to 4 hours to dry out. Once the scales are dry, begin making the gelatin.

For the gelatin and assembly:

Heat ¼ cup of the water until it is hot but not boiling and put it in a small bowl or pitcher. Sprinkle the gelatin over the hot water. (*Note: for the gelatin to dissolve properly, it is important that it's added to the water and not the other way around.*)

Stir until the gelatin has completely dissolved. If the gelatin does not dissolve completely after a minute or so, put the bowl or pitcher in a saucepan of warm water to heat it gently and continue to stir. Once dissolved, put to one side. Stir it occasionally to ensure it doesn't set.

Heat the remaining water in a small saucepan until it is hot but not boiling. Add the sugar and stir until dissolved. Decrease heat to low, add the gelatin mixture, and stir to combine.

Transfer to a heatproof pitcher and add a small amount of both gel food colorings to turn the mixture a pale blue-green. Let mixture cool for a few minutes, stirring occasionally to ensure that it doesn't set.

While the gelatin is cooling, transfer the fondant mermaid scales to the cheesecake. A toothpick can be helpful to make small adjustments to the scales' positioning.

Once the gelatin is lukewarm to the touch, it is ready. Use a teaspoon to place it onto the top of the cheesecake. Do this gently so as not to displace the scales. Once you have a thin covering of gelatin over the whole cheesecake, transfer it to the fridge. (*Note: you probably won't need all the gelatin mixture*.) Leave for 4 to 6 hours, or overnight, to set.

Once the gelatin has set, remove the cheesecake gently from the pan. Bring to room temperature to serve.

🐚 SEAFOAM MOUSSE 🐚

Whip up this creamy dessert for your guests and watch them savor every mouthful!

Serves: 4 🐚 Time: 15 minutes 🐚 Difficulty rating: ⭐

INGREDIENTS

* ½ teaspoon unflavored gelatin powder
* 2 tablespoons cold water
* 1½ cups heavy cream
* 1¾ cups confectioners' sugar, divided
* 2¼ cups cream cheese
* ½ teaspoon peppermint extract
* Green gel food coloring
* 7 ounces dark chocolate (minimum 70 percent cacao), finely chopped
* Whipped cream, in a can
* Four squares dark chocolate, for garnish
* Fresh mint leaves, for garnish

EXTRA EQUIPMENT

You will need an electric hand mixer and four large wine glasses.

METHOD

Add the gelatin to a small bowl with 2 tablespoons water and set aside for 5 to 10 minutes.

Pour the heavy cream into a large bowl and whip until it forms soft peaks, then add ¼ cup of the confectioners' sugar and whip until it forms stiff peaks. (*Note: be careful not to overbeat your cream as it will split.*)

In another bowl, beat the cream cheese with an electric hand mixer until smooth and fluffy, then add the remaining 1¼ cups confectioners' sugar and mix until combined.

Add the peppermint extract and a drop of green gel food coloring to the cream cheese mix to give you a light, mint green shade, and mix.

Heat the set gelatin in a microwave on full power for no more than 30 seconds, or in a small saucepan over medium heat. Whisk to ensure it dissolves. Let cool slightly for 2 minutes, then pour the gelatin mixture into the cream cheese mixture and blend it thoroughly with the hand mixer.

Add the cream and sugar mixture and almost all of the finely chopped chocolate to the cream cheese mixture, and gently fold it in until evenly combined. Spoon the mixture into your serving dishes. Use large wine glasses or any glass or serving dishes suitable. Chill in the fridge for 3 hours or overnight.

Spray the canned whipped cream over the top and garnish with fresh mint leaves, a square of chocolate, and the remaining chopped chocolate to serve.

🐚 UNDER THE SEA POPSICLES 🐚

Cool down on a hot summer's day with these refreshing and fizzy frozen treats.

Makes: 4 🐚 Time: 15 minutes 🐚 Difficulty rating: ⭐

INGREDIENTS

* ★ 1 kiwi fruit
* ★ Handful of blueberries
* ★ 1 cup lemonade
* ★ Turquoise gel food coloring

EXTRA EQUIPMENT

You will need a pitcher, a four-slot popsicle mold, and four popsicle sticks.

METHOD

Cut the kiwi fruit into thin slices and stick one slice onto one side of each popsicle mold. Put some blueberries at the bottom of the molds.

Put the molds into the freezer so the fruit freezes against the sides.

Pour the lemonade into a pitcher, add a drop of the turquoise gel food coloring, and stir.

Remove the molds from the freezer and fill each with the blue lemonade.

Position a popsicle stick in the center of each popsicle mold, then put them back in the freezer.

The popsicle sticks will rise with the bubbles, but after 20 minutes when the mixture has begun to set, you can readjust them and leave the mixture to freeze completely.

To remove the popsicle, warm up the molds with your hands and gently twist and pull the popsicles up and out.

Eat immediately.

🐚 TROPICAL SWISS ROLL 🐚

Dig out the deck chairs, play some calypso music, and feel fully relaxed as you enjoy this slice of food paradise.

Serves: 6–8 🐚 Time: 2 hours 🐚 Difficulty rating: ★ ★

INGREDIENTS

Cake

* 3 eggs
* ⅓ cup superfine sugar, plus 2 tablespoons extra for dusting
* ⅔ cup all-purpose flour
* Zest of 1 lime

Lime curd filling

* ⅓ cup plus 2 tablespoons superfine sugar
* 2 tablespoons butter
* 2 eggs, lightly beaten
* Juice of 2 limes
* Zest of 1 lime
* 1 (13.66 ounce) can full-fat coconut milk, chilled in the fridge and unshaken
* ½ teaspoon vanilla extract
* ¾ cup confectioners' sugar

Decorations

* Lime zest
* Coconut flakes

EXTRA EQUIPMENT

You will need a jelly roll pan or a 9 by 13-inch rimmed baking sheet and an icing spatula.

METHOD

For the cake:

Preheat the oven to 325°F and line a jelly roll pan or a rimmed baking sheet with parchment paper. Set aside.

In a large bowl, whisk together the eggs and superfine sugar for about 5 minutes, until the mixture is pale, thick, and the consistency of mousse.

Sift the flour and add the zest into the mixture and gently fold them in—take your time with this as you don't want to lose any air.

Spread the mixture out into the lined pan using an icing spatula and bake for 8 to 10 minutes. Remove when the cake is a pale golden color and slightly springy. Let cool for 5 minutes.

When it is cool enough to touch, sprinkle an extra 2 tablespoons of superfine sugar over a fresh sheet of parchment paper and quickly flip the cake onto the paper, peeling the lining paper away from the cooked cake.

While it is still warm, carefully roll the cake (from the short end) using the parchment paper as support to lift it, then let cool in the rolled-up position.

For the filling:

Place the sugar, butter, eggs, and lime juice in a saucepan and melt together over medium heat.

Simmer the mixture gently for 10 to 15 minutes, whisking frequently, until it becomes a thick curd.

Pour the curd through a strainer into a bowl, then stir in the lime zest and let cool.

To make the coconut cream, scoop the chilled coconut cream from the top of the can of coconut milk into a bowl and leave the liquid behind. Add the vanilla extract and confectioners' sugar, and mix until creamy and smooth.

To assemble the Swiss roll:

When the cake has fully cooled, unroll it and spread out a layer of half the coconut cream on top, followed by a layer of the lime curd.

Gently re-roll the cake and then spread the remaining coconut cream across the top and down the sides.

Finish with a sprinkle of coconut flakes and lime zest, then cut the ends off to neaten and transfer to a serving plate. Eat within 24 hours.

⚜ CORAL FRUIT TARTS ⚜

One taste of these tarts and you'll be transported to a tropical paradise. If the rain pattering on your window is denying you this vision, just imagine you're a mermaid swimming in the sea.

Makes: 12 ⚜ **Time: 2 hours** ⚜ **Difficulty rating:** ★ ★

INGREDIENTS

Crust

- ★ ⅓ cup plus 2 tablespoons butter, cold
- ★ 1½ cups all purpose flour
- ★ 2 tablespoons confectioners' sugar
- ★ 1 egg, beaten

Filling

- ★ ⅓ cup plus 2 tablespoons superfine sugar
- ★ 1 (8 ounce) package cream cheese, softened
- ★ 1 teaspoon vanilla
- ★ 1 cup heavy cream
- ★ Fresh fruit (kiwi, mango, raspberries, and blueberries)

EXTRA EQUIPMENT

You will need a mini muffin pan, a 2-inch flower cookie cutter, a ½-inch star cutter, a piping bag, a round piping tip, and pie weights or rice.

METHOD

For the crusts:

Preheat the oven to 350°F.

Place the butter and flour in a bowl and mix together with your fingers or a fork to crumble together.

Add the confectioners' sugar and stir, then add the egg and bring the mixture together to form a dough.

Roll the dough out to a thickness of approximately ½ inch, then cut out shapes using the flower cookie cutter until you have twelve flower shapes.

Gently press the shapes into the mini muffin pan holes, and fill each with a small square of parchment paper and a few pie weights or uncooked rice.

Bake for 10 to 15 minutes, checking regularly, until the tarts are lightly golden, then remove from the oven, take out the pie weights or rice, and cool on a wire rack.

For the filling:

In a large bowl, beat the sugar, cream cheese, and vanilla together for 2 to 3 minutes, until creamy.

In another bowl, whip the heavy cream, then fold it into the cheesecake mixture.

Transfer the mixture to a piping bag fitted with a round tip, and fill each tart crust with a generous amount.

Top the tarts with sliced kiwi, star-shaped mango pieces, blueberries, and raspberries, and serve.

You can make the tart crusts and the cheesecake mixture the night before and store them separately to assemble the next day. Keep the cheesecake filling refrigerated and the tart crusts in an airtight container.

Slice the fruit and place it onto each tart right before serving.

DRINKS

❧ MERTASTIC MILKSHAKE ❧

This indulgent sweet masterpiece is one seriously special treat. Let your creativity run wild and serve this chilled drink with a generous dollop of whipped cream, some sprinkles, and a chocolate mermaid tail.

Serves: 2 ❧ Time: 30 minutes ❧ Difficulty rating: ★

INGREDIENTS

* 2 ounces white chocolate
* Pink gel food coloring
* 2 ounces dark chocolate
* 6 scoops vanilla ice cream
* 10 strawberries, hulled and chopped
* ¾ cup plus 2 tablespoons reduced-fat milk
* Whipped cream from a can
* Sprinkles and colorful round candy, for rim and garnish

EXTRA EQUIPMENT

You will need two mermaid tail molds, a piping bag, a small round piping tip, a blender, and two large goblet glasses.

METHOD

Melt the white chocolate in a bowl set over a saucepan of simmering water or in a microwave. Once melted, add a few drops of the pink gel food coloring to the chocolate and mix until it is completely pink. Fill the mermaid molds with the pink chocolate and leave in the freezer to set for 5 minutes.

Melt the dark chocolate in a bowl set over a saucepan of simmering water or in a microwave. Transfer half the dark chocolate into a piping bag fixed with a small round piping tip.

Prepare each glass by piping the chocolate in straight lines, from the bottom to the top of the inside of the glass, then dip the rim in the rest of the melted chocolate and coat it with sprinkles before the chocolate hardens.

Place the vanilla ice cream, strawberries, and milk in a blender and blend until smooth.

Pour into your prepared glass and top with a generous dose of whipped cream and, yes, you guessed it, more sprinkles and colorful candy.

Finally, top with the chocolate mermaid tails.

🐚 SEA BREEZE SLUSHIE 🐚

Feel as cool as a cucumber with this delicately flavored and super-healthy smoothie.

Serves: 2 🐚 **Time: 15 minutes** 🐚 **Difficulty rating:** ⭐

INGREDIENTS

* ★ 1 cucumber, peeled and cubed
* ★ Juice of 1 lime
* ★ 6 to 8 mint leaves, plus more for garnish
* ★ Ice to fill 2 glasses
* ★ Sparkling water to fill 2 glasses
* ★ 2 cucumber slices, for garnish
* ★ Agave syrup (optional)

EXTRA EQUIPMENT

You will need a blender and two large wine glasses (copa glasses are my preferred choice for this drink).

METHOD

Place the cucumber, lime juice, mint, ice, and sparkling water into a blender.

Blend for 1 minute, until there are no large lumps of ice remaining, then pour the drink into the two glasses.

Serve with a slice of cucumber and sprig of mint, and drink immediately.

This is a deliciously refreshing drink, but if you wish to add a touch of sweetener, add a squeeze of agave syrup to the mixture during the blending stage.

✿ LEMONADE FLOAT ✿

When a dip in the ocean isn't possible, this thirst-quenching
classic is the best way to cool down on a hot day.

Serves: 6 ✿ **Time: 15 minutes** ✿ **Difficulty rating:** ★

INGREDIENTS

* ★ ½ cup granulated sugar
* ★ 4¼ cups water, divided
* ★ ½ cup lemon juice
  (about 4 lemons)
* ★ A few handfuls of ice
* ★ 1 tub vanilla ice cream

EXTRA EQUIPMENT

You will need a large pitcher and an ice cream scoop.

METHOD

In a small saucepan, combine the sugar and ½ cup of the water. Bring to a simmer until the sugar dissolves. Remove from the heat and let cool to room temperature.

In a large pitcher, stir together the remaining 3¾ cups water with the cooled simple syrup and lemon juice.

Pour into ice-filled glasses and top with scoops of vanilla ice cream.

Serve with a striped straw and enjoy immediately.

❧ SEALICIOUS CHIA SEED SMOOTHIE ❧

*Keep your energy high and your spirits higher with this morning smoothie,
which can also be turned into a fruity chia pudding, if desired.*

Serves: 2 ❧ **Time: 30 minutes, plus 4 hours 10 minutes cooling time** ❧
Difficulty rating: ★

INGREDIENTS

- ★ 3 tablespoons chia seeds
- ★ 3 cups plant milk (almond, coconut, soy, or oat), divided
- ★ 1 tablespoon honey
- ★ 1⅓ cups frozen blueberries
- ★ 2 (6-ounce) packages strawberries, divided
- ★ 2 bananas

EXTRA EQUIPMENT

You will need a pitcher or bowl, a blender, and two 8-ounce glasses.

METHOD

For the chia pudding:

Pour the chia seeds, 2 cups of the plant milk of choice, and honey into a pitcher or bowl and mix well. Let it settle for 2 to 3 minutes, then mix again until there are no lumps.

Cover the pitcher or bowl and leave in the fridge for 4 hours (or overnight if possible).

For the blueberry layer:

Before taking the chia pudding out of the fridge, prepare your blueberry layer by adding frozen blueberries and ½ cup of the plant milk to a blender. Blend until smooth, then spoon out into your serving glasses, dividing equally. Set in the freezer for 10 minutes.

For the chia pudding layer:

When the blueberry layer has chilled for 10 minutes, remove from the freezer and pour the chia layer on top of the blueberry layer, dividing the mixture equally between the two serving glasses. Slice six strawberries thinly and carefully position them against the glass on top of the chia layer. Put the glasses in the fridge.

For the strawberry/banana layer:

Put the banana and remaining strawberries into a blender with the remaining plant milk and blend until smooth.

Divide the mixture equally between the two glasses and serve immediately.

(Note: turn this into a chia pudding by doubling the amount of chia mixture and splitting half the thickened chia pudding equally between the blueberry and strawberry layer. Layer the flavors as usual but leave them in the fridge to set for an extra 30 minutes before serving.)

MY RECIPE NOTES

CONVERSIONS AND MEASUREMENTS

All the conversions in the tables below are close approximations, which have been rounded up or down. When using a recipe, always stick to one unit of measurement and do not alternate between them.

LIQUID MEASUREMENTS

1 teaspoon = 5ml
1 tablespoon = 15ml
⅛ cup = 30ml
¼ cup = 60ml
½ cup = 120ml
1 cup = 240ml
1 large egg white = 2 tablespoons liquid egg white

BUTTER MEASUREMENTS

1 tablespoon = 14g
2 tablespoons = 28g
¼ cup = 55g
⅓ cup = 75g
½ cup = 115g
⅔ cup = 150g
¾ cup = 170g
1 cup = 225g

DRY INGREDIENT MEASUREMENTS

1 teaspoon = 5g
1 tablespoon = 15g
1 cup flour = 113g for self-rising flour/
              120g for all purpose
1 cup superfine sugar = 225g
1 cup confectioners' sugar = 115g
1 cup brown sugar = 213g
1 cup granulated sugar = 200g
1 cup sprinkles = 192g

OVEN TEMPERATURES

°F	°C
275	140
300	150
325	170
350	180
375	190
400	200
425	220
450	230
475	240

INDEX

ABOUT THE AUTHOR

Alix Carey is a baking enthusiast from Surrey who combined her passions for creativity and writing when she launched her blog, My Kitchen Drawer, in 2015. My Kitchen Drawer is a baking biography showcasing Alix's journey through colorful, fun recipes, baking advice, reviews, and general kitchen-life musings. Alix is a self-confessed dreamer and the author of *The Unicorn Cookbook*.

Follow her on Instagram and Twitter **@mykitchendrawer**.

IMAGE CREDITS

Cover: marble background © tofutyklein/Shutterstock.com; front right photo © Suwapat/Shutterstock.com; all other cover photos © Alix Carey; shells © Alemon cz/Shutterstock.com

Insides: p.23 © Suwapat/Shutterstock.com; p.28 © kiv_ph/Shutterstock.com; p.31—left and middle photos © Ermolaev Alexander/Shutterstock.com, right photo © kiv_ph/Shutterstock.com; pp.34 and 37 © Amy Hunter; p.49 © Elena Schweitzer/Shutterstock.com; p.50 © lenakorzh/Shutterstock.com; p.53 © Claire Berrisford; pp.84 and 86 © Megan Betteridge/Shutterstock.com; p.96 © Iryna Melnyk/Shutterstock.com; pp.112 and 115 © Claire Berrisford; p.126 © mmttp22/Shutterstock.com; all other photos © Alix Carey; shells and starfish © Alemon cz/Shutterstock.com; marble backgrounds © tofutyklein/Shutterstock.com